YOUR STRONGER FINANCIAL FUTURE

The Eight Essential Strategies
for Making Profitable Investments

SMART MONEY-MAKING DECISIONS FOR NOW AND RETIREMENT

YOUR STRONGER FINANCIAL FUTURE

The Eight Essential Strategies
for Making Profitable Investments

MIKE EGAN

New York   Chicago   San Francisco   Lisbon   London   Madrid   Mexico City
Milan   New Delhi   San Juan   Seoul   Singapore   Sydney   Toronto

The McGraw·Hill Companies

1 2 3 4 5 6 7 8 9 10 11 12 13 14 15   QFR/QFR   1 9 8 7 6 5 4 3 2 1

ISBN 978-0-07-177299-0
MHID   0-07-177299-5

e-ISBN 978-0-07-177392-8
e-MHID   0-07-177392-4

This publication is designed to provide accurate and authoritative information in regard to the subject matter covered. It is sold with the understanding that neither the author nor the publisher is engaged in rendering legal, accounting, securities trading, or other professional services. If legal advice or other expert assistance is required, the services of a competent professional person should be sought.
> —*From a Declaration of Principles Jointly Adopted by a Committee of the American Bar Association and a Committee of Publishers and Associations*

Library of Congress Cataloging-in-Publication Data

Egan, Mike
      Your stronger financial future : the eight essential strategies for making profitable investments / Mike Egan.
            p.   cm.
      ISBN 978-0-07-177299-0 (hardcover)
      MHID 0-07-177299-5 (hardcover)
      1. Investments.   2. Finance, Personal.   3. Retirement income—Planning.

      HG4521.E424   2011
      332.6   2011019474

McGraw-Hill books are available at special quantity discounts to use as premiums and sales promotions or for use in corporate training programs. To contact a representative, please e-mail us at bulksales@mcgraw-hill.com.

This book is printed on acid-free paper.

For my dad

Contents

Preface

On December 9, 1989, at the Palazzetto dello Sport in Rome, Italian actress Sophia Loren, beautiful and sparkling with jewelry, grabbed a Ping-Pong ball from a machine that would determine who played host country Italy in the first round of the 1990 FIFA World Cup soccer tournament. The United States' ball was chosen, and immediately fans across the world, particularly those of defending champion Argentina, claimed a conspiracy was afoot. At the time, the United States was not a soccer power. In fact, the country had not played in the World Cup for 40 years. Allowing Italy to play the United States in the first round was like matching LeBron James with a Little League kid for the NBA Slam Dunk Contest.

Yet how could such an event have been rigged? The conspiracy theorists had an answer: Sophia Loren's rings were magnetized, allowing her to grab a certain pre-magnetized ball from the pot.[1] Though most people dismiss this myth, U.S. coach Bruce Arena commented years later on the draws (the opponents selected for the games): "[What] seems odd to me is how the host country gets decent draws." In fact, no host team has ever lost a draw in the first round.

Speculation swirled again in 2006 when German soccer star Lothar Matthäus selected Italy's first-round opponents for the World Cup that year, a daunting group. Sky Italia television claimed the Ping-Pong balls had been heated and cooled, allowing Matthäus to select certain countries that would prove to be difficult opponents.

"The Italians are mad if they think that," said Matthäus.

In regards to the 2006 World Cup Ping-Pong ball theory, University of Michigan professor Andrei Markovits, who wrote a book on such speculation, said, "I hate conspiracy theories. They're an easy way out for people seeking explanations for complex things."[2]

THOSE PING-PONG BALLS ARE WEIGHTED!

Soccer is not the only forum for healthy conspiracy. Wasn't LeBron James, an Ohio native and widely touted high school talent, picked number one in the NBA draft by his hometown team, the Cleveland Cavaliers? Sports conspiracists mull over such theories, as well as why NBA teams representing the larger, more lucrative markets usually get the earliest pick of players during the draft. Others regularly make claims that NBA referees throw games to help certain large-market teams.

But NBA commissioner David Stern has made every effort to quell such speculation. Reporters, independent auditors, and representatives from each of the teams gather in front of the Ping-Pong ball machine before the NBA draft lottery. Everyone must relinquish anything that beeps, rings, or can be used to text or make calls. Even using the restroom requires a security escort.[3]

These precautions, however, do not satisfy the most inquiring minds, who question why this entire process takes place in a private room and not on live television. Conspiracy theories abound on the Internet. Take this sampling from a chat board on the *OnMilwaukee.com* site, posted by someone with the user name brewguru: "It's kind of coincidental that no one ever sees the ping-pong balls come out. They just announce the order and everyone is supposed to take them at their word."[4]

During the infamous 1980 Pennsylvania Lottery scandal, it was discovered that the Daily Number drawing had been fixed by injecting a few grams of white latex paint into several Ping-Pong balls with a hypodermic needle, proving that tampering with Ping-Pong ball drawings is definitely possible.[5] The NBA is confident, however, that Ping-Pong balls and referees are on the level, and Stern keeps improving the process. "We've made great, great advances," he said, "and the conspiracy theories haven't made the same advances."[6]

Backtracking

Alarmist. Foolish. A waste of time by people who have too much time on their hands. That is the assessment of the conspiracy theorists by the sober-minded officials and credible witnesses associated with soccer and the NBA.

But wait. Not so fast.

Professor Markovits, the author who said he hated conspiracies, had to modify his position after revelations of the 2006 Italian professional soccer scandal for match fixing.[7] In one case, a Swiss team named FC Thun lost 5–1 in a game in which they were expected to do far better. According to a Zurich newspaper, an investigation showed players were paid what amounted to $22,000 to ensure their team lost by four goals. "I don't think the draw is rigged," said Markovits, "but I'm less likely to completely dismiss it as a crackpot simplification than I would have been three weeks ago."[8]

Stern Tap-Dances While the Referee Sings

Fans who had been ridiculed for years for their claims of fixed officiating enjoyed new fuel for their conspiracies after referee Tim Donaghy was convicted of affecting the total score of games he personally bet on by how many fouls he called on both teams playing each night. Donaghy did not help matters by claiming a fellow ref said his crew intentionally helped the Los Angeles Lakers beat the Sacramento Kings in game 6 of the 2002 Western Conference finals. In that game, the Lakers shot 18 more foul shots than their opponent in the fourth quarter. Donaghy called these refs "company men" and said they followed the wishes of

NBA executives who wanted more money and TV time from a seventh game in the series. Stern denied the allegation and called the prison-bound Donaghy a "singing, cooperating witness."[9]

SIFTING THROUGH THE PILE OF ACCUSATIONS

Conspiracies are generally suspect. Don't let them distract you from your purpose and your goals. But sometimes they contain a germ of truth. This book seeks to bring to light what is bogus and what is true regarding how the economy affects your financial future.

Acknowledgments

Thanks to the many, many friends who read the manuscript drafts as this book progressed. Thanks also to Dean Arnold, Rob Carr, and Jayme Johnson for their considerable help and expertise. And thanks to my wife, Elise: without your support and patience, I would never have finished!

Introduction

According to extensive research conducted for the National Retirement Risk Index by the Center for Retirement Research, 51 percent of the American population is slated to retire unsuccessfully, a situation also known as being "at risk."[1] The report states several reasons:

- People have been consistently saving less over the past 20 years.[2]
- Traditional pensions are becoming scarce.
- Personal 401(k) accounts are not performing as expected.
- The stock market and interest rates are volatile.
- Health care costs are steadily increasing.
- Life expectancy also is steadily increasing.
- Housing values have plummeted.
- Social Security has been modified for increased taxes and premiums as well as a later payday.

But all those factors are not the real reasons Americans are struggling to stay focused on the critical road to retirement. There are, in fact, strategies in place to overcome these obstacles: professionals are available to provide necessary advice, countless financial vehicles have arisen to meet a plethora of specific needs, and there are resources available if wisdom and discipline are applied to them.

Instead, the real reasons are psychological ones, and there are only two of them. These two reasons—the culprits for causing over half of America to lose the retirement game—are the following: *fear* and *presumption*. These enemies are the opponents this book has resolved to confront in order to help individuals rise to their next level in the quest for financial freedom.

FEAR

"Why worry about the future?"

This is an attitude shared by many Americans as they watch the news on TV and surf the Internet, reading the latest conspiracy theories claiming corruption and collapse at every level of government. The result is apathy. Consider the story of Tennessee Ted:

Ted loves a good conspiracy. He watches the news every day with a skeptical eye. He spends even more time surfing the Internet to find "the real story" behind the news, and he is rarely disappointed. He works for a 300-person company that makes cardboard boxes, and he nets $45,000 a year. He talks with a number of his fellow employees about what he reads on the Internet, and they usually confirm his suspicions: the rich and powerful are out to get the little guys like him.

The Real Story of the Economy

Ted has learned that the Federal Reserve is not a government entity. But he still thinks the Fed is merely a cabal of private bankers that charge interest to the U.S. Treasury for the service of loaning money to place currency in the economy, and that this interest charge is killing the economy, causing inflation, and will eat up any savings Ted happens to accrue.

In Ted's worldview, there is no need for the Fed. The country could just print its own money directly from the Treasury, as the Constitution directs. A couple of presidents tried this, but Ted believes they were killed for the effort.

Ted has given up the idea of getting Social Security in retirement. The country will have collapsed financially by then, and there won't be anything left. Ted is looking over his shoulder, and he wonders if saving for retirement is worth the trouble with such global disasters looming.

Ted's Microeconomy

While Ted loves to talk macroeconomics, he has done little to improve his own microeconomic situation. He doesn't contribute to his 401(k) plan, although his employer has a very generous program in place. He has a family friend who is a Certified Financial Planner™, but Ted feels he gets his best advice from the guys at work. He bought a couple of gold coins in case the economy falters, but on a whim, he also put $10,000 in a growth fund of Chinese stocks. That's where he hears all the action is these days.

Unfortunately, when his wife was diagnosed with cancer, Ted had nothing put away to pay the skyrocketing medical bills. The money in stocks disappeared after the U.S. stock market's 2008/2009 plunge. He was able to cash in the gold for a couple thousand dollars, which hardly helped with the $30,000 in medical expenses. Ted and his wife have $20,000 in credit card bills. They are mortgaged to the hilt with both their house and their two cars. He doesn't know how they will recover from their financial woes, and retirement is such a distant dream he never discusses it.

He's praying for the apocalypse, for more reasons than one.

Stay Focused, Not Distracted

Regardless of where each American stands in his or her quest to retire, none of us needs to be distracted or discouraged by the many conspiracy theories and myths related to money and the larger economy that are circulating in our culture. Rather, each of us needs to stay focused, continue the course, and persevere to the end of this marathon, reaching retirement. The questions this book confronts, similar to Tennessee Ted's concerns, include the following:

- Is Social Security collapsing?
- Doesn't the Federal Reserve keep a percentage of the money that should go to you?
- Why invest in Wall Street with all the corruption?
- Weren't those government bailouts just for the bankers?
- Won't the government provide health insurance to me during my retirement?

Such conspiracy-related questions can easily cause a person to lose motivation. Why continue the disciplines of planning and saving when the systems are corrupt and the future is completely unpredictable?

Are some conspiracy theories true? Yes. In reality, there are many distracting stories, disturbing trends, and conflicting messages out there, and these are often the seeds of the myths that have developed to explain anomalies. Once in a while, a myth ends up being true. More often than not, though, a myth deceptively includes a portion of the truth but overall is not an accurate description of reality.

This book is dedicated to helping the reader wade through the various myths promulgated on radio and TV, in books, and through other media—those theories that not only are false but also encourage honest folks to put their heads in the sand and complain that the sky is falling. Throughout the book, we will dissect a number of these prevalent myths about money issues, on a national and global level, and then separate fact from fiction.

PRESUMPTION

According to surveys, over a quarter of Americans believe they are in good shape regarding their financial future, but in fact, most of them are in real trouble.[3] Perhaps they assume the small percentage of their income set aside each month in their 401(k) retirement account will get the job done. They may also assume the growth stocks in their account will skyrocket. They may have an unrealistic view of the amount Social Security will contribute in the future, or they may presume they will earn a paycheck forever, despite the statistics that say they can't, and won't.

In Strategy #1, we'll tell the story of Wisconsin Rick. Rick is a classic example of presumption. The hope for the first strategy is that Rick offers an effective reality check to those of us tempted to fall into his way of thinking. The desired goal is to move from presumption, to reality, to hope, to action.

YOUR FEELINGS VERSUS THE REALITY

While Americans can be divided into two financial groups, psychologically speaking, they can also be divided into four groups based on how they view their financial situation. These four general groups are defined according to a comprehensive study done by the Center for Retirement Research:[4]

- ◆ Group A (24 percent): Americans who believe they are in good shape and are correct
- ◆ Group B (28 percent): Those who believe they are in good shape and are wrong
- ◆ Group C (33 percent): Those who believe they are in bad shape and are correct
- ◆ Group D (16 percent): Those who believe they are in bad shape and are wrong

Group A, thankfully, is successfully on course. But new trends suggest that retirement is, and will become, considerably more challenging in the future. This group still needs a bit of prodding—encouragement to keep up the pace and increase the focus and discipline that have kept them successfully on course.

The people in Group B, targeted by the enemy called presumption, need to wake up and realize the great challenge before them.

Those in Group C, targeted by fear, already know they are in bad shape. Many of them have been victims of bad information, myths, and conspiracies that have robbed them of the motivation to press forward.

Those in Group D may be pleasantly surprised to learn they are closer to the right road than they realized.

This book provides insight for all four groups. Each section of the book highlights a conspiracy related to money and the economy (the misconception) and then responds by disproving the conspiracy (the truth). Third, and most importantly, each section then ends with practical suggestions beneficial to all of the four groups (the plan). These suggestions remind us about what we need to do personally, regardless of all that frantic chatter in the media—noise that subconsciously encourages us to believe that the traditional road of hard work, discipline, and perseverance is nothing but a lost cause.

Buying into a misconception or myth can move you off course only if you are headed the right way. If you are on the wrong course, you certainly don't need another myth to keep you distracted. Don't fall prey to the conspiracies.

THREE SUGGESTIONS: 20–7–6

Throughout this book, there are numerous detailed suggestions on how to prepare for your financial future. Before we jump into the material, though, I would like to highlight three of the most important items, which are referred to repeatedly. They are straightforward strategies that you should keep in mind when forming the basis of your entire financial plan. These three important items can be summarized and remembered as the expression 20–7–6:

◆ **20:** In Strategy #3, you will learn that the quick way to calculate the savings "number" you need to retire is to multiply the current amount of money you spend each year by 20. (Don't use your pretax or even after-tax income, but only the amount you spend.) The result is your number.

- ◆ **7:** Try to avoid all debt. When you purchase a house or take out a student loan or business loan, never finance the loan longer than seven years.
- ◆ **6:** The amount you need to store up in an emergency fund for your household is six months of income, available for when trouble inevitably arises.

If you can follow the rule of 20–7–6, you will find yourself a long way down the road to financial freedom. This rule goes hand in hand with the first strategy presented: overcoming the misconceptions and charting your own course.

Overcome the Misconceptions and Chart Your Course

THE MISCONCEPTION: YOU'RE ALREADY PREPARED TO RETIRE

According to the National Retirement Risk Index, millions of Americans believe they are successfully headed down the road toward retirement, but their self-assessments are dead wrong. These Americans come in all types and stripes, but for the purposes of an example, let's look at the story of Wisconsin Rick. (This example is fictitious but based on reality.)

Wisconsin Rick sold his electrical-supplies company five years ago, ending up with $8 million in liquid assets. He placed over 90 percent of his portfolio in high-risk growth stocks. Why such a gamble? Simply because Rick has a high risk tolerance and is a confident man. At age 47, he is a mover and shaker around town, plays golf every day at a posh country club, owns a lovely cabin overlooking Lake Michigan, where he enjoys his 58-foot yacht, and eats at the finest restaurants. He's a pretty smart guy, and he made a lot of money selling electrical supplies, primarily cords and adapters. As with many characters like Rick, he is occasionally correct but never in doubt.

Three different times, however, one or more of his financial advisers or friends warned him to diversify his portfolio. His accountant brought it up first, but Rick rebuffed him. His attorney, a golf buddy, also mentioned diversification, but the discussion never went any further. His investment adviser then suggested that Rick might want to consider some bonds and other more conservative securities, but Rick reacted with even more blind confidence, saying, "These high-risk stocks will continue to double every year."

When his net worth dropped from $8 million to $4 million only two years after Rick sold his company, his advisers warned him once again. Later, when that $4 million dropped to $2 million, his accountant actually begged him to consider a change. Though he had no financial plan, Rick insisted the stocks would go right back up. He did not know his final destination or why he took great risks with his portfolio, but he trusted himself more than the professionals who regularly dealt with the market.

Today, Rick has $300,000 in liquid assets, but he is effectively bankrupt, as creditors have placed liens on his remaining money. He sold his yacht and his cabin for a loss. His 5,000-square-foot home has a second mortgage. He now plays golf at the municipal course.

You Know What Happens When You Assume

Rick is the poster child for presumption. Although he was successful at making large amounts of money with his business, he never took the time to develop a strategic plan for this money. Rick could have garnered the counsel of professionals regarding how to develop a plan for his financial future and how to invest his assets. Instead, he relied on his gut instincts, which were entirely wrong. Rick knew he had a lot of money in his home equity, and he presumed the housing market would always keep skyrocketing. He had no provisions in his portfolio for the financial meltdown that wiped out his stocks.

A Real Rick

The *Wall Street Journal* provides a true story similar to Rick's.[1] Michael Donahue made his fortune during the dot-com bubble of the 1990s. Donahue watched his personal stock value rise to $448 million a few months after his business-to-business company, InterWorld Corp., made its initial public offering (IPO) in 1999. Until then, the 36-year-old was making $200,000 a year.

What to do? Donahue bought a $9.6 million home in Palm Beach, Florida. So that he and his wife could enjoy the home while working out of New York, he acquired a private jet. A polo enthusiast, he thought nothing about six-figure contributions to the local polo club in Palm Beach. Donahue had joined that very exclusive group in the world known as the centimillionaire club ($100 million net worth or more). But not too long after he had acquired that wealth, the dot-com bubble burst, and Donahue's $448 million fortune plunged to $12.6 million.

Donahue put his house up on the market. "Going up was easy," he said. "But when it starts going down, no one wants to talk to you."[2]

Unlike many others who joined the centimillionaire club thanks to the Internet boom, Donahue saw his stock stay sky-high long enough that he could sell his shares after the lock-up period, the few months' waiting time before owners of IPO stock are allowed to sell it. Unfortunately, Donahue didn't take advantage of that freedom, since the sale of company stock by a top executive creates bad publicity, which he wanted to avoid. Instead, Donahue took out a $14 million loan against his nearly half-a-billion-dollar stock valuation. When the stock dropped, his company stock assets were worth less than the amount he owed.

Donahue had assumed his financial future would be bright, just as Rick was confident that his shoot-from-the-hip strategy would work just fine. If you were able to ask them before financial disaster struck, they would have told you, "Sure, I can retire. No problem."

THE TRUTH: RECENT TRENDS MAKE IT MUCH MORE DIFFICULT TO RETIRE

Michael Donahue assumed. Wisconsin Rick assumed. We all do it to a certain degree. For millions of Americans like Rick and Michael, financial freedom appears to be squarely on the horizon, and the question of retirement needs no deliberation, no professional assistance, and no strategic planning. In reality, the question of retirement requires all three. If Wisconsin Rick had been made more aware of the financial landscape regarding retirement, who knows? Perhaps he would have been more open to advice. Maybe his future would look much better today.

What follows are nine trends or developments to keep in mind in regards to your retirement. Unfortunately, it is too late to share them with Michael Donahue and Wisconsin Rick.

1. Changes in Social Security

Though Strategy #2 will make it clear that Social Security will indeed be there for you when you retire, it is likely to be less than you expected. Here's why:

- The normal retirement age is gradually being increased from 65 to 67. For those who choose to retire at age 62 or 65, a significant portion of the expected check will be missing.
- Through the 2010s, Medicare Part B premiums, subtracted directly from your Social Security check, are scheduled to increase from 9.4 percent to 11.8 percent of your Social Security benefit.
- For those at a high-income level who pay taxes on Social Security benefits in retirement, the levels of taxation will increase with the rate of inflation.[3]

Social Security only replaces 43 percent of income for low-wage workers. The percentage is lower for high-wage employees. That low number is expected to drop even further to 39 percent when the Full Retirement Age process (the increase from age 65 to 67) is completed.[4]

2. The Decline of Traditional Pensions

In the 1980s, traditional company pension plans, not IRAs or 401(k) plans, were the primary source of private pension coverage. Because the choices were fewer and the ability to get money early was more difficult (or impossible), workers tended to have more money awaiting them in the future. The employer enrolled the worker, made the contributions, and invested the money. Typically, the only available decision for the employee was the age at which to retire.[5]

According to a study by the University of Michigan, one-third of all households end up having no pension coverage at all. This estimate is actually a conservative one, compared with the 50 percent figure cited by studies that include public-sector workers, who are more likely to enjoy a pension. For low-wage earners, up to 72 percent don't have a pension![6]

3. 401(k) Plans Are Not Working as Hoped

About two-thirds of the population continues to enjoy private pension coverage, but a large portion of that group is covered by 401(k) plans, not traditional pensions. While the idea of giving employees a host of options regarding their retirement funds is a noble idea, the current statistics suggest real problems with the concept. Employees with 401(k) plans must make several kinds of decisions:

◆ Whether or not to join the 401(k) plan
◆ How much to contribute
◆ How to invest the contributions
◆ How to use the money during retirement

A fifth of eligible employees do not even participate in their employer's 401(k) plan. Of those who do, only about 10 percent contribute the maximum amount allowed.[7] A large number also cash out their funds when they change jobs. For instance, fully 45 percent of employees who changed jobs in 2004 cashed out all their money.[8] Today, the average job tenure is only four years.[9]

According to the Federal Reserve's Survey of Consumer Finances, the typical individual approaching retirement has $78,000 in his or her 401(k). But had a typical worker making approximately $50,000 contributed 6 percent to a 401(k), assuming the company contributed 3 percent, that employee would have accumulated $320,000. That's obviously a much larger number than $78,000. This data suggest that the poor performance of the 401(k) due to the "human factor" is a major concern, adding real risk to those whose goal is a successful retirement.[10]

4. Other Savings: Are There Any?

Statistics show that little saving is taking place in the United States apart from pensions. Seventy percent of at-risk Americans live paycheck to paycheck. Less than 20 percent of Americans have saved more than three months' worth of income.[11] Only 26 percent of Americans report having acquired a nest egg of $250,000 or more at the time of retirement. One survey estimated an average of $60,000 in savings for those about to retire, an amount, when annuitized, that provides only $250 per month.[12]

5. We Have Longer Lives to Finance

When Social Security was launched in 1935, the life expectancy was 60 years for men and 63 years for women. In 2011, those numbers are 76 for men and 80 for women. In a few decades, those figures will rise to 79 for men and 83 for women. (If these numbers seem high, remember that they represent life expectancy from birth.)

Even more revealing are the statistics for Americans who live to at least age 65. In 1935, men who were 65 years old were expected to live to be 71; for women, it was 77. The averages for today are 92 years for men and 99 years for women who are currently 65. By 2080, people who are 65 are projected to live until 102 for men and 108 for women.[13] All those numbers mean that, over time, more and more money is needed for retirement because the span of time that must be financed is increasing.

Also, resources are becoming scarce for a mighty demographic of people hitting retirement all at once. The baby boom generation peaked in 1957, when 4.3 million babies were born. That generation, born from 1946 to 1964, far surpasses in number the generations following. America is aging. According to the Center for Retirement Research, "By 2025, nearly 1 in 5 Americans will be age 65 or over compared to 1 in 8 today."[14]

6. Housing Equity Has Plummeted

For many Americans, their perceived value of home equity was the fallback plan for savings and retirement. Perhaps they had not contributed well to their 401(k) or had not developed other savings options, but their large house was growing in value, and the resulting equity meant real money someday.

All of that has changed. From 2007 to 2009, average house prices dropped nearly 20 percent, while $3 trillion in housing value was lost. During that time, the amount of debt on those houses remained the same. Studies show that fully 43 percent of households aged 65 to 74 still have housing debt.[15] This drop in equity—for some, a complete loss—means many Americans cannot reap a nest egg of cash by selling their home and scaling down during retirement. The idea of a reverse mortgage during retirement years is no longer a viable option either.

7. Rising Health Care Costs

In the Introduction, the figure of 51 percent was given as the percentage of Americans who are "at risk" and unlikely to retire adequately. That figure, however, was calculated *before* factoring in health care costs. When health care costs are included, the number of at-risk Americans leaps up to 61 percent. For Generation Xers, the figure is 68 percent.[16]

While Medicare and Medicaid cover a good portion of health care costs during retirement, retirees still must directly pay many costs, particularly premiums related to Medicare Part B (physician and hospital services) and Part D (drug-related expenses). These premiums and copayments end up costing an average of $3,800 per year for an individual in retirement and $7,600 per couple, according to the Centers for Medicare and Medicaid Services.[17] Along with these costs, over two-thirds of the population over 65 will require long-term care (assisted living, nursing homes) during some point of their lives. Of that group, 40 percent will require care for two years or more.[18]

So how much money is needed to finance the out-of-pocket health care expenses expected during retirement? According to the Employee Benefit Research Institute, retired men need $86,000, and retired women need $126,000.[19] Covering health care costs will prove far more difficult than expected.

8. Bad Investment Decisions

When the Center for Retirement Research updated its figures to account for the 2008 financial meltdown, it adjusted the amount of equities each household owned to 40 percent less than before the crisis.[20] Nearly half of workers age 56 to 65 had 70 percent or more of their 401(k) invested in equities such as growth stocks the year before the meltdown. Conversely, in a separate study, 32 percent of 401(k) participants held no equities. Even more risky, many 401(k) owners invested a large portion of their holdings in just the stock of the company they work for.[21]

This failure to diversify—and, more particularly, the failure to retain a financial professional to diversify properly—has been a major contributor to increasing the at-risk numbers and hampering Americans from successfully reaching their retirement goals. How many Americans were smart enough to make some financial moves before and after the meltdown? A study by the University of Michigan, which evaluated 1.2 million workers involved in over 1,500 retirement plans, showed that over 80 percent made no trades at all during the two-year period of the study. Eleven percent made a single trade.[22]

9. Other Unknown Problems

Like Murphy's Law, any number of challenges can, and will, arise to keep us from making those daily, tough decisions to preserve our financial future. More than three-quarters of at-risk Americans believe they will still be making money somehow after their retirement. But statistics show that only 12 percent of retirees have jobs. While many have good intentions to stay employed and complete their career, working until retirement age, 47 percent of Americans report leaving the office earlier than they had planned. Reasons cited included health problems, disability, and company downsizings or closings.[23]

Conclusion: Retirement Is Achievable but Difficult

For all these reasons, it is important that all of us tempted by presumption take a long and close look at the trends that place us potentially at risk regarding our financial future. We cannot afford to have the attitude of Wisconsin Rick, who felt he knew better than everyone else, thinking he needed no help nor advice. He assumed his assets would somehow make things work for him when it came time to retire. That wasn't the case. But with just a little planning, a little advice, and a little bit of healthy concern about the future, all of us—including the Ricks—can successfully chart our course.

THE STRATEGY: OVERCOME THE MISCONCEPTIONS AND CHART YOUR COURSE

The misconceptions will distract you from a sound financial and retirement plan. Don't let them! The solution to reaching financial freedom at retirement is not easy, but it *is* simple. The six points that follow involve matters of simple discipline and resolve, or involve allowing others more qualified to provide direction in an area where you may not be the expert—simple, but not always easy.

1. Develop an Overall Financial Plan

We all love to be amateur traders. Wisconsin Rick had strong ideas about his portfolio and invested 90 percent in growth stocks. At the golf club, he debated products such as stocks versus bonds, annuities versus real estate. But the real problem with such discussions is not the issue of whether Rick and his friends are qualified and experienced enough to talk about complex financial products. The issue is much more basic: Rick and his friends are not asking the right questions.

"What financial product should I buy?" is putting the cart way before the horse. Instead, these following questions should be asked before any product is even discussed:

◆ Where are you going?
◆ Where are you now?
◆ What is your risk tolerance?
◆ What is the overall plan?

After these questions are answered, a person can then chart a map from current location to destination. Only after that map is completed (a comprehensive financial plan has been created) is a person prepared to discuss and evaluate the myriad of financial products available.

2. Identify the Inflation-Adjusted Amount of Money You Need at Retirement

It is easy to feel like a gerbil on a wheel. According to Thoreau, "Most men lead lives of quiet desperation." Perhaps that is because they are not exactly sure why they are working so hard. They don't have even a vague notion of the goal.

Although a professional process is advised for determining how much in assets you need to acquire in order to retire successfully, there is a quicker way to do this that will help you get a general sense of your final goal. How much money do you need to retire? (Remember the 20–7–6 phrase.) The answer is what some in the industry refer to as "the number," and at its most basic, it can be described as 20 times your annual spending. We'll discuss this calculation, and its caveats, in detail when we look at Strategy #3.

3. Retain a Licensed Financial Professional

It is imperative that you develop a plan around basic-premise questions and answers that define your core needs before you consider financial products. Developing such a plan is difficult, especially for someone who does not have the appropriate level of financial expertise. Who can help you with this important and complicated process?

A number of licensed professionals in the financial industry are easily available. Once they have helped you draw up a financial plan, they are then able to help you with the complex task of choosing investment products and diversifying your portfolio.

Consider this: Would you perform an appendectomy on yourself? Would you represent yourself in a major lawsuit? Like doctors and lawyers, certified financial professionals are experts in their field. They are critical when approaching the matter of your personal financial future.

4. Develop a Personal Emergency Fund

As cited earlier in this chapter, more than 80 percent of Americans have not put aside even three months of income for a rainy day. Typically, you won't get behind in your finances when everything is going well. The credit cards get used and serious problems begin, however, when times are financially tough or a crisis emerges, whether that means you find yourself unemployed or the economy experiences a major, and potentially long-lasting, recession. By these points, it is too late to save up enough money to get you out of the hole. To avoid ending up at the mercy of the economy or your job status, store up over time a liquid, cash fund of six months' worth of income, the 6 of 20–7–6 discussed in the Introduction. That secret weapon will forgive a multitude of sins when problems arise down the road.

5. Instead of Accruing Debt, Store Up Savings

Debt is the enemy. Except in very limited instances—an affordable house, a two-year car loan, or perhaps a student loan with a promising salary at the end—multiyear financing arrangements are best avoided like the plague. Credit cards will destroy your financial future faster than any other quick fix available. Stop the debt.

Never take out a loan, including for a house, for longer than seven years (there's the 20–7–6 again). That's right, seven years. This will be explained further in Strategy #6. Rather than accruing debt, you must accumulate savings. This single principle will guard you from major financial problems.

Make sure you are allocating the maximum amount to your 401(k) account and, if you work for an employer that "matches" or offers some contribution, that your employer is contributing. Remember to check your statements regularly to verify that the numbers are correct. See to it that the assets in your retirement funds are properly invested. Also, it is always good to consider cutting costs where possible in order to increase savings. Of course, sometimes there is just not much left to squeeze, so instead, figure out potential ways to earn more money.

6. Consider Annuities to Overcome Longer Life Expectancy

As indicated earlier in this chapter, we are living much longer today than our parents and grandparents did. How does this affect our portfolio?

Annuities—investments that provide a fixed amount over a set number of years—provide a strategic role in confronting the financial realities of longer life. But how long will that be? Longevity insurance, an annuity that promises to send you a monthly check for as long as you live, is a product to consider. Another important product during these days of an aging America is long-term care (LTC) insurance. If you are one of the two out of three Americans who will find themselves in a nursing home or assisted-living facility one day, LTC insurance will help cover the bill.

STRATEGY #1 Checklist

☑ Determine your retirement goals.

☑ Develop a financial plan with a financial professional to achieve your retirement goals.

☑ Start saving money, and stop accruing debt.

☑ A good starting point is the 20–7–6 rule.

Develop an Overall Financial Plan of Which Social Security Is Only One Part

THE MISCONCEPTION: SOCIAL SECURITY IS ON THE BRINK OF COLLAPSE

Many Americans have a romantic view of the origins of Social Security: Families gathered around the large radios in their living rooms each week to listen to the encouraging words of President Franklin Delano Roosevelt during the 1930s Great Depression era, preceding the crisis of World War II. Everyone in those days was well aware of beggars on the streets and old people left destitute because of the country's financial woes, but "A chicken in every pot" was a famous promise at the time.

Perhaps the most popular of FDR's New Deal initiatives during the Depression was the establishment of a program to ensure that the elderly would never go penniless. The "Social Security" fund would take 1 percent of each worker's pay from the employers and place it in a closely guarded pot of money, squirreled away for the future, to care for the aged. At least, that was the idealistic notion.

Decades later, that pile of money reserved for the elderly has been raided by the U.S. Congress to pay for big government programs. The new payroll taxes—less controversial than income taxes—have grown from 2 percent to over 12 percent.[1] Also, this money has not all gone into the Social Security pot as the promised chicken was supposed to. Rather, the cook has been tearing off bits of meat and passing out pieces to his friends before the meal ever gets to the table.

By 2016, less money will be collected for Social Security than is supposed to be paid to retirees. If the country experiences more financial crises, the bulk of America's elderly might find themselves with little to no Social Security money in their mailbox each month.

Why work so hard, paying so much in Social Security taxes, if nothing will be available for us when we retire? Why even prepare for retirement at all? The whole process seems futile. Is the Social Security program a scam?

The Pot of Money Is Gone

In 1969, Congress enacted a law that allowed the extra money in the Social Security pot to be used by the federal government to pay for all the programs that income taxes, gas taxes, and other levies couldn't cover. Raiding the chicken in the pot was easier than raising taxes on the people who reelect Congress every two years. This arrangement, in which Social Security's savings were being used to reduce the deficit, was given the tame name of "the unified budget."[2]

When President Ronald Reagan was elected a decade later, he called on his top economic adviser at the time, Alan Greenspan, to solve a serious issue regarding Social Security: when the Baby Boomers hit retirement age in the 2010s and 2020s, the far-less-numerous generations still in the workplace would not be able to fund all those retirees. (Up until that point in history, the younger generations in America had always outnumbered their elders.)

In 1981, Greenspan put together a bipartisan blue-ribbon panel of 15 notables. Bob Dole and Daniel Patrick Moynihan provided senators from the Right and the Left, and other well-known figures like union leader Lane Kirkland added prestige to the panel. Greenspan's solution was to increase the payroll tax percentage, slightly lower Social Security benefits, and gradually increase the age of retirement in a few decades from 65 to 67. These changes brought massive surpluses into the Social Security Trust Fund. Instead of just living paycheck to paycheck, Social Security was now in a position to oversee a pot of money to pay for the retirement of future generations, a scenario most Americans believed was always the case, but which had stopped being the reality for many years.[3]

Greenspan's blue-ribbon panel was not, however, able to demand the immediate separation of the Social Security Trust Fund from the general federal budget. The 1980s were a decade when the federal deficit was a high-profile political issue, so the panel agreed to keep the "unified budget" for another eight years. Then the trust fund could finally be separated from the general budget and acquire a pot of money for retirees.[4]

This never happened, of course. Congress and the president looked the other way, and there was no public outcry to stop the technically illegal process of looting Social Security.

Credible Voices Indict the Scheme

During the tenure of Reagan's successor, George H. W. Bush, Democrat Senator Ernest Hollings of South Carolina addressed the Social Security scandal directly, calling it a "systematic and total ransacking of the Social Security Trust Fund in order to mask the true size of the deficit." Said Hollings, "The promise was that today's huge surpluses would be set safely aside in a Social Security Trust Fund to provide for Baby Boomer retirees in the next century. Well, look again. The Treasury is siphoning off every dollar of the Social Security surplus to meet current operating expenses of the government."[5]

Greenspan later called the raiding of the trust fund "most improper," and Senator Moynihan called it "thievery." Nevertheless, the raiding continues to this day and carries with it an ominous prognosis.[6] Not only does Social Security have no savings—just a paycheck-to-paycheck practice of paying benefits to the current elderly as the current laborers cough up their payroll taxes—the paycheck is about to get a lot smaller. The Social Security Board of Trustees announced in 1990 that more money will be spent than collected as early as 2020. The trustees' 2009 report changed that estimate to 2016.[7]

In February 2010, news reports announced that the future had arrived: in 2010, Social Security spent more than it received. *Fortune* columnist Allan Sloan used numbers from the Congressional Budget Office to show a $28 billion deficit for 2010. "Until this year, Social Security was a problem for the future," said Sloan. "Now it's a problem for the present."[8]

Haeworth Robertson, Social Security's chief actuary from 1975 to 1978, adds another credible voice, confirming that the alleged trust funds are "stark naked; there is nothing in them that can be used to pay future benefits." If something isn't done soon, later attempts will be "frantic, disorganized, and futile."[9]

CNBC's Jim Cramer calls Social Security "the largest Ponzi scheme ever."[10] A Ponzi scheme eventually collapses, as Bernie Madoff's scheme in New York did. Madoff's clients lost their money, as will America's retirees. The federal government, however, will not go to jail. With Social Security poised to collapse, why focus on retirement, savings, and financial planning? Is there simply no point?

THE TRUTH: SOCIAL SECURITY IS AS SECURE AS THE DOLLAR—EVEN MORE SECURE

The truth is that Social Security will not collapse.

It is also true, however, that the pressure of entitlements on the federal government—Social Security, Medicare, Medicaid, welfare, and the weight of military spending—could arguably cause a great financial decline in the United States, especially when taking into account the interest payments required to fund all these growing entitlements. Fully two-thirds of the current federal budget is already slated for entitlements (mandatory items), but Social Security is the largest of those items, at 23 percent of the entire federal budget.[11]

Recipients of Social Security will continue to get their checks. The promises are too etched in stone. And these elderly "customers" are among the most dependable voters in the country. Politicians will therefore always make sure Social Security checks arrive on time. They may have to inflate the dollar to make all these payments, but Social Security payments are indexed to inflation. Lots of the United States' creditors may suffer from a falling dollar, but Social Security recipients will only see their payments rise.[12]

In that sense, Social Security will not collapse. Because of this fact, it is critical that future retirees make every effort to receive their Social Security checks upon retirement and that you, as a future retiree, know the exact amount of your monthly check. What percentage will this amount be for the total monthly income stream required upon your retirement? What kind of serious planning and strategizing have you undertaken regarding your investments? How do your investments incorporate your Social Security income in the grand scheme of your retirement plans?

The truth is that you can count on Social Security providing a portion of your retirement; it will still be there. But the amount you receive is likely to be just a small portion—much less than half—of what you will need to successfully retire. The rest you must obtain through properly invested savings.

You can expect the federal government to take three actions related to Social Security, each of which affects your financial future:

1. Raise the Age for Receiving Social Security Benefits

There are two short-term solutions for keeping the budget balanced due to the rising number of retirees appearing on the scene: raising taxes or cutting costs. Both of these are always politically unpopular. Some of both may occur as solutions, but not likely at a level to solve the massive Social Security imbalances.

The solution will be to do what Greenspan did in the 1980s: increase the retirement age. Actuarially, it is easiest just to say, "OK, you don't retire anymore at 67; you retire at 69." That seemingly small adjustment ends up making a difference of trillions of dollars. Most importantly, raising the age of retirement is relatively painless for your representatives and senators. For younger and middle-aged people, the change is so far away it doesn't really register. (Or maybe they'll just put their heads in the sand like ostriches and pretend old age will never hit them.) The current recipients of Social Security, the ones who would scream if their entitlement were reduced or taken away, would not be affected by this change.

2. Use the Current Social Security Surplus to Hide the Deficit

The explanation at the beginning of this chapter does accurately describe how Congress uses the Social Security surplus to hide the size of the annual deficit each year for the entire budget. We need to make clear, however, that Congress has not taken the entire pot of money, *just the surplus*. (More surpluses are expected in the future; the deficit in 2010 has been explained as being a result of the recession.[13]) In other words, all the money needed to cover payments to retirees was specifically available for that purpose. And all the money in the pot to pay for retirees years down the road is also guaranteed.

Let's use some metaphors. If you put $10 in your bank account each month, at the end of the year, you have $120 in your account.

It's not sitting in a drawer, though; the bank may have loaned out $110 of it. Nevertheless, you can still go get it. The bank will hand you the cash because the bank has promised to do so. It may get the money from another depositor, or if it has to close down, it may get the money from the Federal Deposit Insurance Corporation (FDIC). But your money is guaranteed, even when it is being used for another purpose. The same situation is true for Social Security. The money may not be physically there sitting in a drawer labeled "trust fund" at this moment, but it is very much guaranteed.

Think of the situation this way: Why is a green piece of paper called a dollar worth anything in the first place? Because the federal government says it is. It is backed by "the full faith and credit of the United States government." Similarly, all future Social Security recipients have their retirement income coming to them, promised by "the full faith and credit of the United States government." In other words, your Social Security payments are as certain as the usability of the U.S. dollar. Both are IOUs issued by the federal government.

So Congress has not swiped money from the Social Security account. It has taken the excess money and used it to show that the overspending each year isn't as bad as it seems. For example, in 2007, the federal budget deficit was $152 billion, right?[14] No, it's actually $341 billion if you do not include the Social Security surplus.[15] Not considering the Social Security surplus in the overall deficit is certainly misleading, and it affects the way we view the health and solvency of our government. But the guarantee on the promises to pay future Social Security recipients is solid. Those IOUs are as strong as if piles of greenbacks were stored somewhere for the payments.

3. Inflate the Dollar to Pay Unpaid Bills

Using the Social Security surplus the past 25 years to cause the annual deficit to look smaller creates a much larger problem: temptation for the U.S. government to spend well beyond its means, leading to more and greater deficits. If the annual budget is $1 trillion and we spend $1.1 trillion, where does the extra $100 billion come from? The Treasury borrows or prints the extra money (or changes the digits on a computer screen). This situation devalues the dollar.

Let's use a more extreme example. What happens when the budget doubles to $2 trillion but only $1 trillion worth of money is coming into the government coffers? That second trillion is also simply borrowed or printed by the Treasury. (The deficit part of this example has become a reality. The Obama administration's deficit for the 2009–2010 fiscal years was $1.42 trillion.[16]) In this case, it is easier to see that a dollar becomes worth half its value. Since there are twice as many dollars in the economy, a loaf of bread will require $2 instead of $1. The purchasing power of the dollar has therefore been cut in half, affecting our trading relationship with other countries and their currencies. We can buy only half as much of what we used to from Japan. Germany can buy twice as much of our goods for the same number of Euros.

Conclusion: Social Security Will Not Collapse

In review, Social Security as a program will not collapse. You can be sure you will get your payments down the road. Because of the fact that Social Security is indexed to inflation, you will have the same purchasing power, expressed as a percentage of your income, as you would if your payments began arriving today.

However, because of the massive amount of debt in our country related to entitlements such as Medicaid, Medicare, and Social Security (some estimates as high as $64 trillion[17]), the country as a whole is in danger of economic hardship. In other words, Social Security might finance, say, 40 percent of your retirement 20 years in the future, just as it does for many retirees today. But, in 20 years, that other 60 percent may be nearly impossible to obtain, if in fact the economy as a whole and the value of the dollar have severely declined.[18] Ironically, in 20 years, it may be that Social Security recipients are the only people whose income stream has not collapsed!

THE STRATEGY: DEVELOP AN OVERALL FINANCIAL PLAN WITH SOCIAL SECURITY AS JUST ONE PART

The journey from here to there can be enjoyable, even pleasant, if you know where you're going. Social Security will be there when you retire. But it won't be nearly enough.

How much will it be? How much income per month do you actually need when you retire? What age is best for your retirement? What should you be investing in now based on what you will need on retirement day?

All of these important, basic questions need to be answered in conversations between you and your financial advisor as part of developing a comprehensive financial plan. As previously mentioned, it is terribly premature to discuss stocks, bonds, or other strategic investment vehicles until you have answered the basic questions underlying your investment needs.[19]

Many believe that all wealthy people overseeing millions of dollars in their portfolio have taken tremendous efforts to strategically determine how to manage their assets. Think again. Investment advisers and other financial professionals can tell endless stories regarding incredibly wealthy people who have done little to nothing in planning on how to handle their money.

The example of Wisconsin Rick in Strategy #1 may seem a bit extreme, but his case is not uncommon. More importantly, he reflects a large majority of Americans who do not believe they need a comprehensive financial plan to inform all the other decisions they make regarding their portfolio. Before you buy particular securities and make strategic investments, you need to ask the following major questions.

Question #1: Where Are You Going?

Before you head on a journey, before you develop your map, the very first question to ask yourself is this: "Where am I going?"

Rick did not really know where he was headed. He knew he liked to make a lot of money, and he loved doubling his portfolio. He also had high risk tolerance. But he had never really asked himself, "How much is enough?" or considered what to do with his life when he made all the money he was chasing. With some sober reflection and a solid plan, Rick, with the help of his advisers, could have hedged his assets as he reached his destination.

The factors related to answering this question of your exact destination involve the following information:

- How old are you now, and at what age do you plan to retire?
- What do you desire or expect your monthly income to be when you do retire?
- What do you desire to be the value of your estate, if any, when you retire?

Without an answer to the key question of where you are going, you can't competently chart an investment strategy. In addition, you must consider several more questions.

Question #2: Where Are You Now?

If you are headed somewhere in your car, you have to prepare for the trip by consulting a map or other navigation system. You must identify two key spots: where you are headed and where you are currently located. Financially, to determine where you are, you need to compile three lists, including the value of each item:

- A list of everything you own (including items such as your house, 401(k), investments, and savings)
- A list of everything owed to you (including items like Social Security and an expected inheritance)
- A list of everything you owe (such as credit cards, mortgages, and auto loans)

Question #3: What Is Your Risk Tolerance?

Can you stick with an investment decision, or will the fluctuations of the market and the chatter of friends and family cause you to change course? If the latter is true for you, then you likely have a low risk tolerance. Wisconsin Rick had a high risk tolerance, but most people are in the middle. Where you personally fall in this continuum is another key factor that should influence how a professional financial plan will be constructed to fit your specific needs.

Question #4: What Is the Plan?

Only after the first three questions are answered can anyone, amateur or professional, begin the process of developing a retirement plan. Many people, like Wisconsin Rick, dive right into Question #4, picking various interesting and technical investment products for their portfolio. But falling for that temptation places the cart before the horse.[20]

To develop the plan, you should get qualified and professionally certified help. Strategy #4 will detail who can help you in developing a solid, comprehensive financial plan, but for now, it is important to know that you must consult a licensed financial professional such as a Certified Financial Planner™ (CFP®).

First, Get Your Social Security Secured

Our discussion of the critical importance of developing a comprehensive financial plan grew out of the fact that Social Security will indeed be alive and well at the time you retire. But since it will not be nearly enough, you need a larger plan to reach your goal.

However, you'll need to take some very practical steps to ensure that you do, indeed, receive your Social Security payments upon retirement. It is actually possible that you could get lost in the system and fail to receive your payments if you do not register.

But how do you ensure that your contributions are being tracked correctly? There is a simple solution. Go to the Social Security Administration's website (http://www.ssa.gov/estimator) and use the retirement estimator. When you enter your personal information, the website will estimate your benefits based on your Social Security earnings history.[21] Not only will you be sure that you qualify for Social Security benefits, you will also have useful information for your financial adviser.

The Social Security retirement estimator provides key benefit information. Most important, your ability to access it guarantees you are in the system. Sometimes a clerical error might get a name wrong or miss the Social Security number by a digit on your statement. It happens. You want to get that corrected now rather than the day you retire. It is probable that if you waited and later found out you have a problem, you could hire an attorney, but you would have to go through a lengthy, expensive process to prove that you worked and made your Social Security payments. Wouldn't it be easier to just check now and make sure that the information is correct?

Besides confirming your basic information, the retirement estimator from Social Security will document how many quarters you have paid into the system. The golden number is 40, or 10 years. Reaching this golden number means that at retirement, you will be provided with the full amount you are rightly allowed to receive each month from Social Security. If you reach your 10 years by age 30 and never work again, you will still receive your full payments when you retire.

If you are a nonworking spouse (if you have not worked for at least 10 years but are or were married to someone who did), you will receive your deceased or divorced spouse's payments, if he or she did in fact work 10 years or more and if you were married to him or her for 10 years or more and he or she reached retirement age or dies. It is important to check now to make sure the documentation is correct. The Social Security system in regards to this situation is interesting: If a man had four wives, each for 10 years or more, all four will receive half his Social Security income after his retirement! (Elizabeth Taylor, married eight times, had only one spouse eligible to receive spousal benefits—Richard Burton.[22])

Accessing your information on the retirement estimator serves another good purpose: it provides documentation of an "asset," as you get from any bank statement or investment statement you receive regularly.

By reviewing your report available online, you can easily obtain an estimate from Social Security regarding the benefit you will receive when you reach age 62, 67, or 70. This information is extremely helpful in providing a sense of how much money you will need to save in order to retire at the level appropriate for you.

STRATEGY #2 Checklist

☑ Meet with a licensed financial professional such as a CFP®. Develop a retirement plan.

☑ Make sure you are registered in the Social Security system.

☑ Review your retirement plan with your financial professional at least semiannually.

Identify the Inflation-Adjusted Amount You Need at Retirement

THE MISCONCEPTION: THE FED SKIMS 5 PERCENT FROM OUR CURRENCY, CAUSING INFLATION, WHICH RUINS OUR SAVINGS

Some people say the history of America turned for the worse in 1910, when seven men representing seven giant bankers met to devise a scheme at a vacation mansion owned by J. P. Morgan on Jekyll Island, Georgia. In attendance were the decision makers for the fortunes of John D. Rockefeller, J. P. Morgan, and a handful of the richest men in America and Europe. The goal of this great rivals' meeting was to unite and conquer the banking system by creating a central bank in the United States, an entity responsible for creating and printing the country's money. The bankers planned to increase their already large fortunes by charging the country interest for creating this money.

YOUR STRONGER FINANCIAL FUTURE

In December 1913, their scheme was successfully accomplished when President Woodrow Wilson helped pass the Federal Reserve Act over the Christmas weekend. The central bank created by this act was named the Federal Reserve. It had no reserves, just the authority to print money whenever desired, and it was not, in fact, federal. This central bank in America is owned by private bankers. These private bankers are known to make a fortune by charging Americans interest on their own money.

Inflation Destroys Our Savings

Since the Federal Reserve was created, the purchasing power of U.S. currency has decreased to four cents on the dollar.[1] The Fed can print as much money as it wants, and it has done just that, since the dollar is no longer connected to a gold standard. In 1900, all dollar bills stated that they were redeemable in gold or silver. You could take a dollar to the bank and get a gold coin in return. That system has ended. The Fed no longer needs to worry about the existence of enough gold to back all the dollars it prints. So it has printed trillions of them. When it does, the value of a dollar continues to diminish.

Columnist Pat Buchanan describes the decline of the dollar: "In 1913, when the Fed was created with the duty of preserving the dollar, one 20-dollar bill could buy one 20-dollar gold piece. Fifty 20-dollar bills are needed today to buy one 20-dollar gold piece. Under the Fed's custody, the U.S. dollar has lost 98 percent of its value."[2]

"My father bought his house in 1954 for $27,000, in Long Island, in a very wealthy neighborhood," said Hollywood producer Aaron Russo, who created a documentary exposing the Federal Reserve. "We were middle-class. That house just resold again, I was over to visit it, and the guy just bought the house, paid over a $1 million for it. The value of that house has gone up about 50 times in 50 years. That's because they print so much money."[3]

"Inflation has been used to pay for all the wars and empires," says Congressman Ron Paul, a longtime opponent of the Fed.

"Debasing a currency is counterfeiting; it steals value from every dollar earned or saved."[4]

How can we "save" for retirement when no one knows what inflation will do to our savings?

By some estimates, the entire unfunded obligations of the United States are approaching $65 trillion, which amounts to a dizzying $547,000 of government debt per household.[5] If the entire assets of America are $44 trillion, the country has over $30 trillion in unsecured debt to private banks such as those that own the Federal Reserve. Nearly a fifth of the current U.S. budget each year goes to paying interest to the bankers, which could increase to over half the budget if present trends continue.[6]

Banks and Ben Franklin

The U.S. Constitution gives Congress the power to coin money, and when the U.S. Treasury creates money directly, no interest is paid to a bank. So why does our government today spend unnecessary money on interest to a central bank when it can print its own money directly? Because central bankers want to get rich from controlling the banking system.

The United States has endured a long history of central bankers seeking to insidiously worm their way into the coffers of the U.S. government. Sometimes these bankers have failed, and other times they have succeeded. It was the prosperity of the American colonies in the mid-1700s, gained in large part from their own paper money called "colonial scrip," that caused the British Parliament and the Bank of England (that country's central bank) to become jealous and covetous of a portion of Americans' prosperity.

"In the colonies, we issue our own paper money," Benjamin Franklin wrote in the mid-1700s. "We control its purchasing power, and we have no interest to pay to no one [sic]."[7]

After independence, Franklin goes so far as to say that the Revolutionary War was about the creation of money, not about taxes: "The colonies would have gladly borne the little tax on tea and other matters had it not been the poverty caused by the bad influence of the English bankers on the Parliament, which has caused in the Colonies hatred of England and the Revolutionary War."

Such quotes imply that what led to the war wasn't the taxes themselves, but England's demand that colonists pay them only in British currency, not colonial scrip. "The refusal of King George to allow the Colonies to operate an honest money system, which freed the ordinary man from the clutches of the money manipulators, was probably the prime cause of the Revolution," concluded Franklin.

After the successful American Revolution, chaos and trouble during the 1780s led Alexander Hamilton, the first secretary of the treasury, to propose a central bank for America. Thomas Jefferson and others bitterly opposed the idea. "I believe that banking institutions are more dangerous to our liberties than standing armies," said Jefferson. "If the American people ever allow private banks to control the issue of their currency, first by inflation, then by deflation, the banks and corporations that will grow up around [the banks] will deprive the people of all property until their children wake up homeless on the continent their fathers conquered."[8]

Jefferson lost the battle, and George Washington approved Hamilton's bank. But he added a proviso that the bank must automatically expire in 20 years.[9]

This first central bank expired on March 3, 1811. Some historians claim that Britain's invasion of America in the War of 1812 was over the United States' refusal to renew the central bank's charter, which was partly owned by English banks, including the well-known Rothschild banking empire.[10] These same historians say the Rothschild bank funded Britain's war effort. (Bank founder Mayer Amschel Rothschild is famous for his cynical statement "Give me control of a nation's money supply, and I care not who makes its laws."[11])

Andrew Jackson Bitterly Opposes a Central Bank

President James Madison, who opposed the original bank bill with Thomas Jefferson, printed money directly from the Treasury, interest free, to fund the war against the British. But later in his second term, Madison agreed in 1816 to a bill establishing the Second Bank of the United States. When this bank neared its expiration date 20 years later, central banking again became the most important issue in the nation. Andrew Jackson ran on the campaign slogan, "Jackson and NO Bank!" In 1832 Jackson kept his promise and vetoed Congress's bill to renew the bank's charter.

Perhaps the most important and famous issue in Jackson's two-term presidency was his fight against central bank leader Nicholas Biddle. "The bank," Jackson told his vice president, Martin Van Buren, "is trying to kill me, but I will kill it."[12]

In 1833, Jackson instructed his treasury secretary to stop depositing U.S. funds in Biddle's central bank. The secretary refused and was fired by Jackson, as was this treasury secretary's replacement. The third secretary followed Jackson's orders.

Jackson was quite vocal against Biddle and the bank: "You are a den of vipers and thieves. I have determined to rout you out, and by the Eternal (bringing his fist down on the table), I will rout you out."[13]

In his final year, Jackson presented a budget that paid off the entire debt of the United States, leaving no interest payments for the people to pay to the bankers. No president before or since has done this. Jackson killed the central bank.

A few weeks later, Richard Lawrence attempted to assassinate Jackson with two pistols, but he failed. Lawrence later said wealthy friends in Europe put him up to it, but since he was acquitted by reason of insanity, few paid attention to his allegations.[14]

Lincoln Just Says No to Interest

A period of great prosperity followed Jackson's heroic efforts, but a few decades later, the Civil War crisis tempted Abraham Lincoln to pursue massive amounts of money from bankers. The Rothschild banks in Europe demanded 24 to 36 percent interest, so Lincoln decided to print money directly from the U.S. Treasury. These "greenbacks," as they were called, successfully financed the war but angered the bankers.

"Government should create, issue, and circulate all the currency," said Lincoln. "Creating and issuing money . . . will save the taxpayers immense sums of interest, and money will cease to be the master and become the servant of humanity."[15]

A newly reelected Lincoln was not expected to use interest to finance the postwar boom, but the country was unable to confirm this plan. On April 14, 1865, Lincoln was assassinated by John Wilkes Booth, a man with strange connections to the Knights of the Golden Circle, a secret society claimed by many to include well-connected bankers on both sides of the Atlantic.[16]

The Real Government Is the Fed

Central bankers finally obtained their ultimate dream in 1913, when a cartel of private bankers known as the Federal Reserve convinced Congress to pay interest to banks again in order to print their money. Their charter was, and remains, endless, unlike the 20-year charter President Washington insisted upon to check the power of the banks. The Federal Reserve has continued with its monopoly for almost 100 years.

"What's happened in America is that the corporations have taken over," says filmmaker Aaron Russo, "and the largest corporation of all is the Federal Reserve System. People don't think of the Federal Reserve System as being a corporation. They think it's a government agency, and it's not. It's a cabal, it's a partnership between the government and this private bank."[17]

Some current members of Congress believe the role of government has become almost insignificant in light of the heavy-handed role played by the Fed in the economy, and the Fed's refusal to reveal to which banks it lends money.[18] In 2008, after Congress went through a grueling process to agree to the Troubled Asset Relief Program (TARP) bailout of $700 billion, it came to light that the Fed had put in place trillions in bailouts, making the government's activity rather paltry.[19]

"We spend hours and hours arguing over $10 million amendments on the floor of the Senate," said Senator Bernie Sanders of

Vermont, "but there has been no discussion about who has been receiving this $3 trillion. It is beyond comprehension."[20]

Longtime congressman and presidential candidate Ron Paul is one of the few high-profile elected officials to call for an end to the Federal Reserve. In 2010, he also persuaded a majority in the House of Representatives to support his bill calling for an audit of the Federal Reserve (H.R. 1207, the Federal Reserve Transparency Act of 2009).[21] Currently, no one but the private bankers know where the money goes. The Federal Reserve bailout figure, as of December 2008, was about $5 billion. The combined U.S. government and Federal Reserve bailout figure is now estimated to be over $8 trillion.[22]

"When [Fed Chairman] Ben Bernanke quickly refuses to give us information about the trillions of dollars of credit that he recently passed out in the bailout process because that would be 'counterproductive,' he is really saying, 'It's none of your business,'" said Paul.[23]

In addition to calling for an audit of the Fed, Paul makes no secret of his ultimate goal: it is the title of his bestselling book, *End the Fed*. "The Federal Reserve should be abolished because it is immoral, unconstitutional, impractical, promotes bad economics, and undermines liberty," writes Paul. "Nothing good can come from the Federal Reserve. It is the biggest taxer of them all. Diluting the value of the dollar by increasing its supply is a vicious, sinister tax on the poor and middle class."[24]

Even Woodrow Wilson, the president who helped rich bankers pass the Federal Reserve Act during that ominous Christmas weekend in 1913, in a campaign speech just one year earlier, expressed his doubts regarding private bankers controlling the nation: "A great industrial nation is controlled by its system of credit. Our system of credit is privately concentrated. The growth of the nation, therefore, and all our activities are in the hands of a few men who, even if their action be honest and intended for the public interest, are necessarily concentrated upon the great undertakings in which their own money is involved and who necessarily, by very reason of their own limitations, chill and check and destroy genuine economic freedom." Wilson went on to lament his country falling under "the duress of small groups of dominant men."[25]

This small group of "banksters," as critics now describe them, is keeping average Americans from being able to successfully save and retire. Inflation caused by the Fed destroys the value of savings, and the amount needed to retire continues to be an unknown, moving target.

Who will stand up for the average American? No president in over a century has challenged the Federal Reserve directly or attempted to print money directly from the Treasury, with one exception. John F. Kennedy, five months before his death, issued Executive Order 11110. This decree returned to the U.S. federal government the constitutional right to create and "to issue silver certificates against any silver bullion, silver, or standard silver dollars in the Treasury."[26]

As a result, $4,292,893,815 worth of new "Kennedy Bills" were created through the U.S. Treasury instead of the Federal Reserve System, meaning the private banks owned by the Fed received no interest from the Kennedy Bills. In 1964, however, President Lyndon B. Johnson's secretary of the treasury, C. Douglas Dillon, stopped the redemption of the Kennedy Bills, thereby stopping the executive order.

THE TRUTH: A CENTRAL BANK HAS POSITIVES AND NEGATIVES

Neither establishing a central bank nor abolishing the Federal Reserve will solve the United States' financial woes. It would be nice if the global plight were that simple. In reality, our lives and the economy are much more complicated than pointing at one institution and calling for its demise, as if this silver bullet could end our economic struggles. Besides, George Washington and Alexander Hamilton founded our nation's first central bank. Were they evil?

It's true that Thomas Jefferson strongly opposed a central bank, and Benjamin Franklin had his own criticisms of the Bank of England. However, the quotes by Franklin in the preceding section, popular on the Internet, are in fact misquotes. The false quotes are likely derived from the following true quote, attributed to Franklin when he was questioned by Parliament as to why the colonists were upset:

> To a concurrence of causes: the restraints lately laid on their trade, by which the bringing of foreign gold and silver into the Colonies was prevented; the prohibition of making paper money among themselves, and then demanding a new and heavy tax by stamps; taking away, at the same time, trials by juries, and refusing to receive and hear their humble petitions.

As you can see, Franklin listed central banking as *one of several* reasons for the colonial uprising, not "the prime cause of the Revolution," as he is sometimes misquoted.[27]

John F. Kennedy's executive order to issue silver currency might raise an eyebrow, except for the following facts: The president was already able to issue such currency; JFK simply granted that same power to the secretary of the treasury. And LBJ never actually reversed the order; Ronald Reagan finally reversed it in 1987 as a general cleanup of executive orders.[28]

The Fed Visits McDonald's

The concept of a central authority monitoring the flow of money derives from a basic principle relative to economic production. Let me provide an analogy in which the only products that can be purchased are McDonald's hamburgers.

In this closed economy, 100 people work at McDonald's. They each make $1 a year. With that dollar, they purchase a hamburger, which costs a dollar. (In this example, a person apparently needs only one burger a year to survive. Work with me.) So the entire economy in this closed system has a gross domestic product of $100.

The following year, an innovative worker figures out how to tweak the machines so they can produce 110 hamburgers. All the employees, however, still work the same number of hours. What is the result? Since no more money has been introduced into the system, those hamburgers will cost less, approximately 91 cents each.

Now, if you are a smart worker at McDonald's, and you know you are going to buy a hamburger that year, would you buy your burger right away? No, you would wait until the surplus burgers are produced and the price has gone down.

This lowering of the burger price is known as deflation. Deflation causes consumers to slow down or stop their purchasing. On a massive scale, this deferment of consumption causes an economic recession as the whole economy or population waits for a cheaper tomorrow. And if the currently produced burgers do not get purchased right away, the manager tells workers to stay home. Unemployment rears its ugly head. Deflation is horrible for a consumption-oriented society. (And, by the way, most of the developed world is consumption oriented.)

Now let us suppose that we could introduce a central bank into the McDonald's closed economy, which is out of balance with 110 burgers made per year but only $100 in the economy. What if the central bank added another $10 to the economy? What would happen? People might go back to paying $1 for their burger. Or perhaps they might pay 90 cents and save the 10 cents for something else. Perhaps ketchup or a pickle has been made available.

As production, innovation, and money get added to the system, then perhaps products like french fries, sodas, or ice-cream sundaes get added to the menu. So if productivity goes up and it is exactly matched by the increase in the money supply, you end up with a happier population, because they get more for the same amount of money. And deflation is avoided.

What about inflation? Inflation occurs when a central bank adds more money to the economy than is needed to match the growth in productivity. If the central bank added $100 to the McDonald's economy, then instead of stimulating the process, it would create a situation where the burgers would cost twice as much.

Finding the Balance Between Inflation and Deflation

Clearly, neither deflation nor inflation is a desired goal. In America, we have tended to agree on moderate (1 to 2 percent) inflation per year as a tolerable fact of life.

The Federal Reserve System was created in 1913 after decades of wild swings in the market, steep periods of inflation and deflation, and numerous runs on banks that left customers penniless, unable to get their money back. During those years, the United States saw as many as 30,000 types of currencies flowing through the banks of the country. Every little bank in every town might issue its own currency. Even the local drugstore could issue its own form of scrip.

The Federal Reserve System resolved to end much of the volatility associated with so many currencies and the ups and downs of the market. By creating a central authority and a common standardized currency, the Fed introduced a system that provided to depositors a guaranteed place to put their savings. The Fed also introduced a central committee to make careful, deliberate decisions regarding the expansion and contraction of the money supply, based on concerns about inflation or deflation.

It's true that the Fed is not exactly an agency of the U.S. government. Neither is it completely a private entity, however, as seven of its twelve directors are appointed by the president (with the consent of the Senate), as is the Fed's chairman. The Fed is actually a public-private partnership, a unique entity accountable to both the private and public sectors.

Does the Fed make a nice profit from the government for issuing its money, as so many people assume in our discussion of the misconception? No. In fact, the Treasury Department charges the Fed four cents for every dollar printed and sent to the Fed for distribution.

It is true that the Fed collects interest from the securities it buys and sells on behalf of the Treasury Department, in order to finance debt. This revenue, along with the normal fees a bank would charge for transactions, is what finances the operation of the Federal Reserve. And while the figure can be a large one (in 2007 it was $42 billion), historically over 95 percent of all the Fed's revenues have been returned to the U.S. Treasury. The Fed pays its bills and returns the surplus to the government. In 2008, that figure was $31.7 billion.[29]

While it is entertaining to quote legendary European banker Mayer Amschel Rothschild with the statement "Give me control of a nation's money supply, and I care not who makes its laws," that quote is another of the many outright misquotes circulating in cyberspace. This attribution to Rothschild, born in 1744, does not appear until 1935. The quote appears to derive from the old English proverb "Let me make the songs of a nation, and I care not who makes its laws."[30]

Similarly, the quotes of Woodrow Wilson in the previous section also are misleading. Wilson's lamenting about a few dominant men and a system of credit destroying the economy were made in 1912, before he signed the Federal Reserve Act. Wilson believed the Fed was the answer to problems about which he was complaining.[31]

The Fed Is Audited, but Let's Audit It More

So why all the ruckus these days about the Federal Reserve? Like any monolithic institution, the Federal Reserve could probably use more oversight and accountability. While the Fed is not the source of all our problems, it most definitely could benefit from some adjustments in its operations.

Congressman Ron Paul's call for an audit of the Fed (H.R. 1207) certainly has merit, as evidenced by the overwhelming number of representatives who have signed on to the bill. However, the truth is that the Fed has always been audited and continues to be audited by the Government Accountability Office (GAO) each year.

Actually, "the Fed is quite forthcoming about its activities," says *HousingWire* columnist Linda Lowell:

> On a weekly basis the Fed reports "Factors Affecting Reserve Balances of Depository Institutions and Condition Statement of Federal Reserve Banks" (Statistical Release H.4.1, easily found on federalreserve.gov). In addition, there are System Monthly Reports on Credit and Liquidity Programs, and a variety of reports pursuant to Section 129 of the Emergency Economic Stabilization Act of 2008: regular updates, updates specific to AIG, Bank of America, Bear Stearns, Citigroup and the various emergency funding facilities. Then there's a massive annual report. This includes an independent audit—by a Big Four audit firm—of the system. The Federal Reserve also has posted readable explanations of its programs and the data they produce on its website. It's not sexy stuff, but it represents a sincere attempt to dispel the mystery and misunderstanding about Fed operations.[32]

These audits go a long way in dispelling conspiracy theories surrounding the Fed. Nevertheless, there is merit to Ron Paul's assertion that the key item not audited in the Fed's activities is its transactions with foreign nations. Paul quotes a GAO official: "We do not see how we can satisfactorily audit the Federal Reserve System without authority to examine the largest single category of financial transactions and assets that it has."[33]

Like any institution, the Federal Reserve has its positives and negatives. More accountability and more creative ways to audit the Fed are good ideas, but more scrutiny—or even abolishing the Fed, as Paul is calling for—will not be the silver-bullet solution to

America's financial problems. It took us a few decades to get here, and it will likely take us a good while to return.

THE STRATEGY: IDENTIFY THE INFLATION-ADJUSTED AMOUNT YOU NEED AT RETIREMENT

Rather than worrying about how much the Fed is skimming from the currency, we are all better off finding ways to skim 5 or 10 percent from our paycheck each month to increase our retirement nest egg. The Fed is not criminal, and it does not skim 5 percent from the currency. It does, however, attempt to monitor inflation. The truth for you is that inflation is a part of our current reality. As citizens and taxpayers, we should work to ensure that our monetary system, with or without the Federal Reserve, is serving our country honorably and with as little inflation as possible. But as an investor, you must take inflation seriously and account for it carefully in your plans.

One hundred years ago, many people did not own stocks and bonds. They owned their house. They owned farmland. They may have owned a factory, but that was how they made their living. If the factory burned down, they lost everything. When insurance became more popular, factory or farm owners were able to retain their assets. But since they did not own a portfolio of hard assets, what happened when inflation soared? They could only hope that the value of their factory would increase and the value of the products they manufactured kept up with inflation. For them, it was one egg in one basket.

Today we all need to own assets that will grow as inflation erodes the value of the dollar. You need to determine your personal "number" with inflation in mind. Lee Eisenberg's book called *The Number* pounds home the case that it is extremely important to have a specific monetary goal for your retirement.[34] It is too easy to say, "I will just save as best I can and hope that the pile I have when I stop working will do the job." You may find that the pile needs to be much larger than you thought. And there may be strategic ways to handle that pile as you get closer and closer to retirement day.

What Is Your Number? A Factor of 20

What specific amount of money do you need to reach in order to retire successfully? How do you determine that number?

Twenty. Your number is 20 times the amount of money you are spending this year. If you are living on $50,000 this year, then your number is $1 million. If you are living on $200,000, your retirement number is $4 million. There are three guidelines to consider:

1. Do not multiply 20 by your gross income. For example, if you make $100,000 a year but $40,000 goes to taxes and you save $10,000, then you are spending $50,000. Your number is $1 million ($50,000 after taxes and savings × 20).
2. Your number, the pile of money you need to retire, does not include Social Security and also does not consider the effects of inflation on your non–Social Security assets. When added together, these two will at worst cancel each other out.
3. Your savings should be held in liquid assets—not in your business, not in the value of your home, not in the peat moss in the backyard.

The formulation of your number assumes you have no other debt and the mortgage on your house is paid in full. (Also, you don't owe your brother-in-law or other family member.)

Remember 20–7–6 as a Guide to Your Financial Future

Remember, the expression 20–7–6 discussed in the Introduction communicates a broad strategy for reaching your retirement goal:

◆ **20:** As just explained, 20 is the multiplier of your annual spending that enables you to determine your number—the amount of money you need to retire.

◆ **7:** This is the number that keeps you out of debt. This did not sound crazy a century ago, but today you should not take out a mortgage or incur any other debt for which the payoff is longer than seven years. If you can't buy the house with a seven-year note, find a smaller one or rent a home. This rule of 7 will greatly help in keeping you debt free come retirement day. (Strategy #6 goes into detail concerning this rule.)

◆ **6:** This number keeps you from dipping into your retirement funds. As detailed in Strategy #5, every smart investor keeps six months of income handy in a separate emergency fund. When unexpected crises occur, you are ready to bail yourself out without resorting to credit cards or to raiding your own retirement funds.

20–7–6 will take you across the goal line!

Your Number Should Not Include Home Equity

Many people believe they will solve a large part of their retirement challenge by accumulating equity in their home. This has proven to be a difficult path. Therefore, you should not include home equity when calculating your number or following the 20–7–6 rule.

"On balance, the higher mortgage debt almost completely cancelled out the positive impact of higher home prices," wrote the Center for Retirement Research in 2007, "leading to no change in the 'at risk' status of Early Boomers, Late Boomers, or Generation Xers."[35]

Counting on home equity looked a lot better in 2007, when the Dow reached 14,000 and housing prices were near their all-time high. However, two years later, after the fall 2008 meltdown, housing values fell nearly 20 percent. Overall, housing values dropped $3 trillion, and direct equity holdings of households plummeted by $7 trillion.[36]

Many aging Americans had counted on a reverse mortgage to fund their future lifestyle. Instead, they found themselves with large mortgages continuing to loom in their futures. A *Wall Street Journal* article reports that 43 percent of households aged 65 to 74 continue to shoulder housing debt.[37]

At the same time that housing values crashed, the mortgage debt on housing—which was significant—has remained fixed. Americans now have little home equity but continue to owe significant housing debt.[38]

Withdrawal Rate

Many academics and financial professionals dedicate considerable amounts of time to determining the "best" withdrawal rate for retirees. In other words, how much money do I take out of my nest egg each year after I retire? Mathematicians and engineers crank out all sorts of numbers and publish the results in trade magazines. The subject can become complex, because some years the market goes up 30 percent—you can withdraw quite a bit that year! Other years, obviously, the market goes down.

To simplify the matter for this book, I suggest a withdrawal rate of 5 percent each year because it is appropriate and simple. (The experts generally provide figures between 4 and 6 percent when determining a withdrawal rate over a 30-year period.)

The 20 figure recommended in this book provides a number that is actually a bit more than you need. So if 6 percent is the best withdrawal rate, you will still be OK. The extra buffer provided by the 20 number will also help with inflation. And Social Security is not included in the formula, so several buffers keep you covered while you work on the simple formula: 20 times your annual expenditures this year, followed by a 5 percent withdrawal rate each year for the remainder of your life.

How should the nest egg you are building over time be invested? This is a subject you should discuss with your adviser, but many financial practitioners suggest using an estimated 8.5 percent annual return. That number is consistent with the performance of investments over the decades, despite the ups and downs of the market. Your portfolio may include bonds, cash, and stocks—and the stocks category often may include real estate, commodities, private equity, venture capital, hedge funds, and other alternative investments. Annuities may also be a part of the portfolio. The tax on your investments should be around 1 percent. That brings you down to a net 7.5 percent upon retirement.

Inflation? Who knows what inflation will be in 20 years? Who knows what the rate will be tomorrow? One percent? Two percent? A reasonable figure is 2.5 percent each year. So, subtract 2.5 percentage points (inflation) from your 7.5 percent (after-tax portfolio return). Now you are at 5 percent, the very amount you will have available to withdraw each year when you retire.

You are likely to never run out of money using this formula. In your first few years, you may find yourself spending a bit more than you do when you are 85 and older. You may simply need less as you get older: octogenarians rarely dole out money for new golf clubs and running shoes. Of course, medical expenses do increase greatly as you age. Medicare covers only part of that challenge. Another product to consider is long-term care insurance, an idea that may save you and your children much worry in an age of assisted living and nursing home care.

STRATEGY #3 Checklist

☑ Determine the total amount of money that you will need in order to reach retirement successfully: multiply the amount of money you spend now by 20.

☑ Do not include home equity in your number.

☑ Start saving at least 5 percent of your paycheck for retirement in an effort to reach your retirement goal.

Retain a Licensed Financial Professional Who Deals with Wall Street

THE MISCONCEPTION: WALL STREET IS CORRUPT, SO YOU SHOULD AVOID IT

Wall Street is a place where the little guy gets taken. Instead of losing money in mutual funds, bonds, annuities, and other technical products that are difficult for the average person to understand, the wise will keep their cash safe in savings accounts or bank CDs, piles of cash under the mattress, or a safe in the basement of the house. If the need arises to grow your money through investments, make those financial decisions yourself while avoiding the corrupt players on Wall Street.

You need look no further than one of the largest firms on Wall Street, Goldman Sachs, for a front-and-center example of a firm selling fraudulent products to unsuspecting folks, mostly elderly people. To add insult to injury, executives at such firms then pocket billions in bonuses and other compensation after the products they sell collapse and impoverish their customers.

The Dot-Com Bust

During the Internet craze, Goldman Sachs staked out its position as the world leader of the Roaring Nineties, underwriting initial public offerings (IPOs) that led to its paying over $150 million in fines or settlements for the alleged fraud involved.[1] Goldman Sachs made tens of billions in annual revenues in the 1990s, and the investment products in which the firm transacted resulted in profits for everyone involved—except perhaps the firm's customers.

The Internet boom was an unusual time. Up until the 1990s, Goldman Sachs and other investment banks enjoyed a decent reputation for refusing to underwrite and promote suspect securities to their customers, which were largely insurance companies and pension funds that managed millions of older people's money. "Since the Depression, there were strict underwriting guidelines that Wall Street adhered to when taking a company public," says one high-profile hedge fund manager. "The company had to be in business for a minimum of five years, and it had to show profitability for three consecutive years. But Wall Street took these guidelines and threw them in the trash."[2]

The requirement was lowered to requiring a firm to show profit for at least a year, and then just a quarter, according to University of Florida finance professor Jay Ritter. "By the time of the Internet bubble, they were not even requiring profitability in the foreseeable future."[3]

Many of the hundreds of IPOs underwritten by Goldman featured unprofitable companies, and that included 14 of the last 18 companies that Goldman rolled out before the Internet bubble burst. These companies "weren't much more than pot-fueled ideas scrawled on napkins by up-too-late bong smokers . . . and sold to the public for megamillions," according to acerbic investigative reporter, and regular *Rolling Stone* contributor, Matt Taibbi.[4]

Some of Goldman's clients filed lawsuits accusing the firm of driving up company prices through undisclosed practices called "laddering." *YourDictionary* defines laddering as follows:

> A practice of initial public offering (IPO) underwriters that requires investors to buy shares at higher prices in the after-market as a condition for receiving lower-priced shares of the IPO. Following the stock market bubble that burst after reaching historic highs in early 2000, laddering has been mentioned as one possible explanation for the unique run up in first-day trading prices of IPOs during the bubble. Some IPOs even made triple-digit one-day gains.

Goldman and friendly institutional customers made backroom agreements to inflate prices through purchasing and repurchasing the new stock as it rose.[5] Goldman pocketed a multimillion-dollar fee from underwriting each IPO and then abandoned its customers when the Internet bubble exploded in 2000.

Goldman later agreed to pay $40 million to plaintiffs for its laddering violations, while at the same time denying any wrong-doing. This settlement, however, was a minuscule amount compared with the billions in revenues made during the boom.[6]

In 2002, a report by the House Financial Services Committee fingered Goldman for another version of Internet IPO fraud called "spinning," described by *Investopedia.com* as "the practice of brokerage houses exchanging IPO shares with top executives for reciprocating business from their companies." Exhibit A was eBay CEO and Goldman Sachs board member Meg Whitman receiving shares of new IPOs underwritten by Goldman at the IPO price. This scheme allowed Whitman to pocket millions that really belonged to the newly public companies and their shareholders. Those millions of dollars should have helped the new companies' profit and loss statements. Instead, the money secured Whitman's promise to use Goldman for eBay's future Internet banking needs—a fortune's worth of business.[7]

In fact, Goldman sold IPO shares to executives in more than 100 stock offerings underwritten by Goldman, including Goldman's own initial stock offering in 1999. The House report included other high-profile recipients of such insider deals, notably Yahoo! cofounder Jerry Yang and infamous Enron CEO Ken Lay. These people escaped punishment. Goldman denounced the spinning accusations as "an egregious distortion of the facts." Then Goldman paid $110 million in settlements and penalties to end the controversy.[8]

After the bust in 2000, the U.S. stock market lost $5 trillion in value, and the NASDAQ was wiped out.[9] Meanwhile, from 1999 to 2002, Goldman Sachs paid out $25.5 billion in compensation and benefits—an average of $350,000 a year per employee.

Reporter Taibbi notes sarcastically that the small fines paid by Goldman several years after the gouging likely did not affect the biggest players, who were "by then, running the U.S. Treasury [Clinton appointee Robert Rubin] or maybe the state of New Jersey [Governor Jon Corzine]." They were no longer associated with the entity being fined and had already gotten their money.[10] "If you laddered and spun 50 Internet IPOs that went bust within a year, so what? By the time the Securities and Exchange Commission got around to fining your firm $110 million, the yacht you bought with your IPO bonuses was already six years old," wrote Taibbi.

Wall Street's Corrupt Housing Scam

After the Internet bust, with the stock market struggling, Wall Street predators were forced to look elsewhere to pry loads of money from unsuspecting customers. They found what they were looking for in the housing market. Once again, Goldman Sachs led the pack.

Goldman used the same strategy as it did for the underwriting of IPOs for unprofitable companies: lower the standards for underwriting. The IPO scam abolished the long-standing underwriting standard of selling investment opportunities in profitable companies. This time, Wall Street extended the sharp decline in underwriting standards to the issuance of bonds backed by residential mortgages. For decades, banks have required that prospective house buyers possess a 20 percent deposit, a steady income, and a high credit score. Now, with subprime mortgages combined with the collateralized debt obligation (CDO), an entity made famous by Goldman, unsuspecting investors could purchase mortgages, as Taibbi puts it, "on the backs of cocktail waitresses and ex-cons carrying five bucks and a Snickers bar."[11]

The older folks in the United States didn't buy these bonds directly. Their pension fund managers did, by the billions. These pension funds are highly regulated, and the government requires that they invest only in safe products such as Treasury bills and cash. But Goldman Sachs and other Wall Street firms somehow convinced credit-rating agencies like Moody's and Standard & Poor's to grade a large "pool" of subprime mortgages as "AAA" (their highest rating, which implies that the bond has virtually no risk of default). These subprime mortgages were piled in with other decent mortgages, which somehow assured the powers that be that the good would outdo the bad in the investment's performance. With that seal of approval, Goldman created billions of toxic, subprime-laden CDOs, and pension fund managers accepted them with delight, as these "safe" investments outperformed all their other boring products.

A decade before Goldman popularized the CDO, early signs of looming disaster emerged from similar strategies. Giants like Procter & Gamble suffered major losses from complex investments. Orange County, California, went bankrupt in 1994. Such debacles led a woman named Brooksley Born, head of the Commodity Futures Trading Commission, to urge the Clinton administration to increase disclosures for CDOs and require higher reserves from banks to sell them.[12] Former Goldman CEO Robert Rubin, who served as Clinton's secretary of treasury when Born blew the whistle, held emergency meetings to stop the proposed regulations. "The banks go crazy—they want it stopped," said Michael Greenberger, formerly one of Born's staff at the CFTC and now a law professor at the University of Maryland. "Especially Rubin."

Born refused to back down, and Rubin publicly opposed her recommendations. Eventually, he convinced Congress to pass the now-infamous Commodity Futures Modernization Act, stripping the agency run by Born of its authority over subprime lending. By the peak of the housing bubble in 2006, Goldman was securitizing over $75 billion in mortgages—a third of them subprime—and selling them to its faithful and trusting institutional customers.[13]

When the bubble burst, Goldman once again found itself in a position of being sued by many of its customers. This time it settled for $60 million, an amount less than the revenues of two days of business during the several-year housing spree. In 2006, the year the bubble burst, Goldman employees enjoyed $16.5 billion in compensation, about $625,000 per employee, while the rest of Americans watched their pensions and home equity plummet.

Gas Prices Rise, Granny's Retirement Plunges

Wall Street does not have a conscience and does not reel from whatever happens to be its most recent plundering. When the housing market plummeted, Goldman Sachs had another bubble waiting in the wings so it could successfully transfer money from the accounts of ordinary Americans and the pensions of unsuspecting senior citizens to the balance sheets of the investment banks.

With stocks and mortgages no longer a safe place for money, investors looked for something more tangible, like commodities—particularly oil. The price of oil jumped dramatically from $60 a barrel in 2007 to $147 a barrel in 2008. During the presidential campaign, politicians proposed solutions to increase domestic oil drilling, but oddly enough, the objective information from the U.S. Energy Information Administration showed that the supply of oil was fine and actually growing, while demand was growing at a lesser pace. Such a situation should result in lower prices, not higher. Once again, however, Wall Street and its biggest firm, Goldman Sachs, led the way to create a new bubble in the market.

Oil had increased so rapidly in price because Goldman Sachs convinced the government that Wall Street firms should be allowed to speculate on commodities and oil. By 2008, a barrel of oil was trading 27 times before it reached its final customer, and total annual oil speculation grew in five years from $13 billion to $317 billion.

As usual, the major customers for Goldman Sachs were the insurance and pension fund managers, who believed this new investment strategy would be safe and lucrative. However, oil prices plummeted from $147 down to $33 in the summer of 2008. The pension funds—including CalPERS (the California Public Employees' Retirement System), which owned $1.1 billion in crude oil investments when the bubble burst—lost mightily. Beyond these pension fund losses, every American was played the sucker for spending over $4 a gallon at the pump for no good reason.[14]

The laws that regulate speculation on commodities were written in the Depression era to protect farmers from losing money if prices fell between the time they harvested their crop and the time they got it to market. A small amount of speculating was allowed, always tying a real buyer to a seller of real, tangible goods. But in 1991, Goldman Sachs somehow persuaded the Commodity Futures Trading Commission (CFTC) that investment banks, just like the farmers of the 1930s, needed protection in case the markets went bad while they held ownership. The CFTC called this the "bona fide hedging exemption," and products like oil barrels went from being traded once or twice to 27 times.

The story of how the bona fide hedging exemption came to light is fascinating in and of itself. No one knew about the 1991 end around until 2008, when a staffer for the House Energy and Commerce Committee heard regulators refer to a letter exempting Goldman Sachs from the traditional commodities speculations: "They start saying, 'Yeah, we've been issuing these letters for years now.' I raised my hand and said, 'Really? You issued a letter? Can I see it?' And they were like, Duh."

This staffer, quoted by Taibbi in *Rolling Stone*, then related how the regulators refused to show him the letter, saying Goldman Sachs had to approve of the disclosure so as not to reveal any market secrets. But since the letter was 17 years old and a bit irrelevant to today's Dow Jones index, the staffer won the day.

Avoid Wall Street and the World of Investing

It is bad enough that Wall Street firms like Goldman Sachs operate in a corrupt manner, giving average Americans the perception they should avoid the market and play it safe with their money. But to add insult to injury, these firms, which make billions and billions of dollars, pay little or no taxes. In 2008, Goldman Sachs paid its employees $10 billion, but it paid just $14 million in taxes. That's a tax rate of 1 percent on its profits of $2 billion and less than a third of what Goldman CEO Lloyd Blankfein made the same year: $42.9 million.

Matt Taibbi sums it up well: "This is the world we live in now. And in this world, some of us have to play by the rules, while others get a note from the principal excusing them from homework till the end of time, plus 10 billion free dollars in a paper bag to buy lunch."[15]

Goldman Sachs wasn't the only Wall Street firm to make a fortune and snub Uncle Sam. According to a report from the Government Accountability Office, two-thirds of U.S. corporations paid no taxes at all from 1998 to 2005.[16]

The rules are different for Wall Street. It's best we all avoid the place. Put your money in safe places. If you have to invest to grow your portfolio, make the decisions yourself, and forget the self-serving brokers who work for Wall Street.

THE TRUTH: WALL STREET PLAYS HARDBALL, WITH NO LEGAL OBLIGATION TO THE LITTLE GUY

It is true. Wall Street does not always look after the little guy, nor is it necessarily supposed to. Wall Street looks after itself and does a pretty good job of it. In contrast with the common misperception, however, Wall Street is *not* corrupt, though it is self-serving and interested primarily in profits—greed, if you will.

The truth for you, the reader, is that the shenanigans on Wall Street must not distract you from your own decisions, your own money, and your own choices with your portfolio. You cannot let "Wall Street" prevent you from wisely growing your investments. Certainly, we must put on another hat as taxpayers and ask specific questions of Wall Street, and we will explore some of those issues in this section, but most importantly, it is imperative to find a way to prosper despite what you see on the news or read online. You must differentiate among those on Wall Street who owe the investor a "fiduciary" duty, those who are subject to a "suitability" standard, and those who have no duty to the investor at all. We will cover these distinctions later in the strategy section of this chapter.

Defining the Players on Wall Street

First off, what is "Wall Street"?

The obvious: Wall Street is a street in New York City, built in the 1600s. The Dutch, who were the first settlers, built a wall next to the street as a rampart to keep out attackers. The British removed the wall a century later, but the name stuck.

In the 1700s, people would gather under a buttonwood tree on Wall Street to trade their goods in what was a glorified flea market. The trading became more and more sophisticated. Eventually, the flea market was renamed, creating the first moniker for the New York Stock Exchange: the Buttonwood Agreement.[17]

Today, Wall Street basically sells money. This transaction happens in various forms, but the overall idea is that people and institutions with money are looking for people and institutions with ideas and ventures that will grow successfully with their financial backing, making more money for both parties. The people working Wall Street connect the money people with the idea people.

Wall Street in New York is not the only place this process happens. There are huge exchanges in Chicago, San Francisco, London, Hong Kong, and many other places throughout the world. Money people and idea people also enter into private transactions at the offices of wealthy investors. A retired couple might invest money with the boy who mows their lawn, who has dreams of owning his own landscaping business. They conduct a "Wall Street" transaction at the couple's kitchen table. So "Wall Street" happens everywhere. But it happens most famously in New York.

Who are the major players on Wall Street?

- **Commercial banks.** People who have saved up their cash are likely to put their money in banks. They do this for three reasons: one, to receive a small amount of interest on their money; two, to have a safe place to keep their money; and three, to have a convenient way of making transactions. The bank guarantees that the customers can take all of their money out of the bank at any time, and the federal government makes the same guarantee, up to $250,000.[18] Once you place your money in a bank account, the bank loans your money to other people and businesses. The business might pay the bank 5 percent for the money, and you may get 2 percent from the bank in exchange for letting the bank use it to fund the third-party person or business. The bank makes money from this arrangement by pocketing the spread between the 5 percent and 2 percent. For instance, a bank may take $100 from a customer, put it in the vault, and then loan $90 to a business. One year later, the bank pays the customer $2 and receives $4.50 from the business. The bank nets $2.50.

- **Investment banks.** Unlike commercial banks, investment banks do not guarantee that their customers will get their money back. An investment bank takes $100 from its customer in return for a piece of paper showing ownership in an enterprise. It may be $100 worth of stock in an established company or $100 of a loan the established company or a government entity promises to pay back (i.e., bonds). Or it may be the first stock ever issued by a new company (an initial public offering, or IPO). Although investment banks do not guarantee to return the $100, they offer investments that could return 25 percent, 50 percent, or over 100 percent—far better than the 2 percent interest from the commercial bank. High risk, high reward. (Goldman Sachs was historically the world's largest investment bank but changed its charter in 2008 to become a commercial bank.)

◆ **Broker-dealers.** A broker-dealer sells and resells the investments created by the investment banks. This setup is known as the secondary market. All the hullabaloo one sees in the pit at the stock exchanges is the broker-dealers buying and selling these investments. The amount of trading in IPOs and other investment bank activity is dwarfed by the secondary market activities of broker-dealers. Institutional broker-dealer firms have gone by recognizable names such as Merrill Lynch, Smith Barney, Morgan Stanley, and UBS. A broker-dealer will take a customer's $100 and might, for example, buy $99 worth of Microsoft stock that has already been bought and sold many times. The broker keeps $1 as a commission and then is off to the next transaction.

Buyer Beware: Wall Street Has No Fiduciary Responsibility to You

The most important thing to note regarding all these Wall Street entities discussed is that they work for themselves and their owners. They do not have a fiduciary responsibility to their customers—meaning, for example, that Goldman Sachs reports to the people who own Goldman Sachs stock. Goldman's job is to make sure its investors are making a good profit, not to make sure its customers make money. True, a good businessperson strives to do both, but there is no *legal requirement* for Wall Street to look after the customers' best interests, just as there is no requirement for beauty parlors to prevent you from getting a bad haircut, or for fast-food chains to serve you healthy food. McDonald's might be out of business if it had a fiduciary responsibility to its customers' health.

Just as shoppers are encouraged to read the label on consumer products, be they food, cigarettes, airline tickets, or anything else, investors are encouraged to read the "label" on investment products. The label is called a prospectus, the paperwork that describes the investment. Wall Street operatives are required to give you that paperwork, but they are not required to tell you whether the investment is a good choice or a bad choice for you.

Goldman Sachs is not a government entity. It does not have a fiduciary responsibility to its customers. Just like the hot dog vendor, it is a business, out to make a profit. You and I can buy shares of stock in Goldman Sachs. If you and I were shareholders, we would want Goldman Sachs to make a lot of money. We would certainly want it to do so in an ethical, law-abiding way. But at the end of the day, we want the firm to make a good profit, or the firm's senior executives are fired. That is the way firms on Wall Street operate.

The public may not like the way Goldman Sachs employees received large bonuses after receiving billions in government bailouts (a subject covered in a later chapter), but shareholders in Goldman Sachs are not that concerned, as long as Goldman is profitable.

Who Drives Up the Market? Hedge Funds

Hedge funds, another type of entity on Wall Street, likely play a larger role than investment banks in artificially driving up the price of the market. A hedge fund is a private investment pool of contributions made by wealthy investors, pension funds, and large financial institutions. Hedge funds are similar to mutual funds in that both aggregate many investors' cash into one "pool," but mutual funds are not discussed much in the media because they are generally boring: mutual fund managers invest in less-complex products and often hold on to them for a long time.

A hedge fund is much more aggressive than a mutual fund and places greater emphasis on leveraging the invested money. For example, a hedge fund manager may go to a bank and say, "I have $1,000 of investor money. Lend me another $1,000." So the hedge fund manager now has $2,000 to invest. If a particular investment rises in value by 15 percent, the gain is $300. However, $300 is 30 percent on the original investor's capital, so the investor is receiving a greater return on investment.

A hedge fund may reduce the risk associated with this leverage, for example, by buying puts (bets that the stock will drop) on some of its investments. If the stock goes down, the fund is covered. For example, a hedge fund might buy one share of Coke but also buy one put on Coke. Or it might buy a share of Coke and simultaneously sell a share of Pepsi.

In the grand scheme of things, hedge funds cause much more volatility in the markets than do investment banks like Goldman Sachs. Goldman might sell a certain amount of initial stock, but then the secondary market and the hedge funds immediately start selling a hundred times more. Now the hedge funds buy 100 shares of Coke and sell 100 shares of Pepsi. If Coke goes up a penny, their clients make a dollar!

This situation becomes highly volatile. Like the other Wall Street players, hedge fund managers have no fiduciary obligation to their customers or to any other market participant.

Calling Wall Street Corrupt Is Like Calling the NFL Too Physical

Is Wall Street corrupt? Of course, there are always crooks out there, and certain players might be fingered for unlawful activity, but in general, Wall Street is simply a collection of institutions doing what they are supposed to do: make money. The people working for the U.S. government and regulatory agencies often do not get paid as much as their Wall Street counterparts, and their ability to keep up with the aggressive Wall Street players will always be hampered. Meanwhile, the sharpest, brightest, and most aggressive minds in the world are working for financial institutions. They are paid to find every little loophole, every quasi-legal opportunity available to make money for their firm. Like hard hitting in the NFL, Wall Street is a major contact sport: it's made for big leaguers, not little guys.

On Wall Street, sophisticated institutions play by sophisticated rules. How is the little guy, the individual investor, supposed to compete with an entire room of Ph.D.s from MIT who program their computers to take advantage of the smallest microshift in trading? He can't. Nobody can. He should not bother to try. Instead, he should entrust his money to an adviser who has a fiduciary obligation to him.

Now, if you want to take a small portion of your money and take a risk, terrific. Find someone connected to those financial institutions, someone who lives and breathes that job, and trade a little bit from your account if you think you have a certain advantage against the market. Turn the rest of your money over to someone who knows your whole story, what you are trying to accomplish, and your short- and long-term financial goals in life, so that person can help you succeed. That's the truth for you. Get some help from someone who has been working the flea market for 20 years and knows all the vendors.

Who Caused the Bailout Crisis?

What about the flea market itself? As a taxpayer, should I be concerned about Wall Street? What should I do?

In regards to the accusation cited earlier in this chapter that a large percentage of U.S. corporations doing business in America pay little or no taxes, this is shockingly and absolutely true. According to the Government Accountability Office, 57 percent of U.S. companies paid no income taxes for at least one year from

1998 to 2005. The GAO said corporations escaped paying taxes for a variety of reasons, including "an ability . . . to shift income to low tax countries."[19]

What about the problem of millions of American investors losing billions in the market from 2001 to 2010? Who is responsible? Goldman Sachs? Perhaps, because that firm and all other investment banks let their high underwriting standards diminish in order to sell more IPOs and subprime mortgages. However, they were never required by law to keep those high standards. The risks were all in the prospectuses, but the public was not necessarily interested in reading them.

You could maybe claim that the pension fund manager who bought these risky investments is at fault. But she could respond, "Hey, I was relying on the credit-rating agencies like Moody's and Standard & Poor's, which gave them AAA ratings!" Then the credit agencies will try to pass the blame, saying, "We were relying on historical data."

Evidence exists, however, that the rating agencies were *not* doing their jobs. According to reports and interviews with JPMorgan bank employees, who were directed by JPMorgan Chase CEO Jamie Dimon to investigate the opportunity for JPMorgan to issue the kind of controversial mortgage-backed bonds that the firm's competitors were issuing, they concluded that the historical data indicated very high risk. The JPMorgan employees scoured historical data and concluded in a report to Dimon that "not enough historical data exists to justify the claims made by our competitors."[20] Dimon directed his bank to avoid participation in these products, and JPMorgan was one of the only banks not to participate in the mortgage meltdown.

Was it the fault of local mortgage loan officers, who knew that borrowers could not afford the loan for a million-dollar house but wrote it anyway? Perhaps it was the fault of the buyers themselves. Aren't buyers responsible if they portray themselves as people who can afford a million-dollar home when they cannot?

One more Wall Street player should be named here as possibly contributing to the bank bailout crisis due to a lack of regulation: private equity.

A good example of private equity is the previously mentioned retired couple who decided to hand their lawn boy a check at their kitchen table to help him start a new landscaping business. Suppose they decide to give him $1,000, but because of their vote of confidence, they convince a bank to loan him another $1,000. Private equity, sometimes known as venture capital, structures these types of loans worldwide with billions of dollars. But the leveraging grows and grows. Instead of the bank giving the lawn boy $1,000, it loans him $99,000.

If the landscaping venture makes a million dollars, the couple might make half a million. But if the venture fails, the couple loses only the $1,000 they invested, and the bank is left holding the bag. When the loans in this kind of scenario add up to billions of dollars, as happened in the recent banking crisis, the taxpayers are forced to bail out these institutions for fear they might implode and cause a run on the banks.

Who Is Really to Blame for the Bailout Crisis?

One candidate for taking the ultimate blame for a spiraling stock market and lost investments is the declining standards of American consumers. A century ago, Americans were far better at saving and far better at inspecting the qualities of the places they put their money. Many of us had grandparents who watched their financial books like hawks, paying for their small houses with cash, if they didn't build them with their own hands. The average mortgage a century ago was paid off in less than seven years. Goldman Sachs operated under scrupulous underwriting standards years ago because its customers demanded that kind of a standard. Today we might be more concerned with watching cable TV and ordering a pizza than with taking care of our financial future, while we let somebody else watch the money.

Can the federal government do a better job than it has of regulating Wall Street? Yes. But it can do just as good a job of holding back Wall Street from correcting its mistakes. When the culture of American consumers increases its discipline in financial matters, both government and Wall Street will be held accountable to clean up their messes. The truth, for you, is to invest wisely, choose proper advisers, and successfully grow your portfolio, despite what happens on "Wall Street."

THE STRATEGY: RETAIN A LICENSED FINANCIAL PROFESSIONAL WHO DEALS WITH WALL STREET

A 2007 study by Charles Schwab illustrates the value of working with a financial professional. It found that 401(k) participants who utilized a financial professional experienced returns of 2.50 percent per year greater than those who did not.[21] It is critical for those who are serious about retirement to hire a professional in the financial world to help them navigate Wall Street. Consider this: Would you operate on your own knee? Would you try to fix the engine in your car? Of course not. Neither should you try to grow your own investments by negotiating with Wall Street all by yourself.

For the past 20 years, mutual funds earned an average of 8 percent. Do you know what the average individual earned by investing in mutual funds during the past 20 years? Only 2 percent.[22] Why? Because individuals tend to buy when the market is hot; then they panic and sell when the market falls. How many of your friends sold at the end of 2008? Most of those investments have earned as much as a 50 percent return since then! A seasoned professional is more likely to keep you from panicking during the regular occurrence of business cycles.

According to a study by GfK Roper, almost half of at-risk Americans say they have "extreme difficulty" when trying to understand financial information. Over half say they believe retirement planning is harder than raising a family. "So where do they go for advice?" asks financial planner Brent Neiser. "Not to professional planners, not to the financial services industry, and not to the media—they rely on relatives, friends, and co-workers."[23]

Resist the Temptation to Confront Wall Street Alone

Just like our friend Wisconsin Rick from Strategy #1, many of us are easily led into the trap of relying on our own instincts to play the market, rather than going to the expert—the doctor or specialist of the financial world. Folks love to discuss the market and enjoy swapping stories about various investments and securities they have purchased and how they perform. We might get tips from our neighbors or friends at the local watering hole. Everybody has an opinion.

If you are one of those people who invest for themselves based on the advice of family and friends, here are some good questions to ask yourself:

- How is that working for you?
- Did you sell when the market dropped and buy when it started rallying again?
- What is your financial plan if you happen to get hit by a bus? Does your spouse or do your kids know what happens in such a situation?
- Do you have a plan that shows each stage of your financial progress and how you need to invest based on each stage?

According to a report by the University of Michigan, most Americans make little or no regular changes to retirement portfolios. Fully 80 percent of those surveyed said they made no changes over a two-year period. Eleven percent made a single trade.[24]

Failure to diversify is one of the major omissions by retirement account owners. A study by Holden and VanDerhei of the Employee Benefit Research Institute in Washington, D.C., shows that 31.6 percent of 401(k) participants have 80 percent of their holdings in risky, growth-oriented equities, while 21 percent held no equities at all. Either position amounts to poor diversification.[25]

Even more risky, a large percentage of 401(k) owners place a significant amount of their holdings in the stock of their employer. In large plans with more than 5,000 participants, company stock accounted for 34 percent of the total assets. According to the Center for Retirement Research, overinvesting by employees in their employer's company stock places a 401(k) in double jeopardy: "If the company does poorly, both current earnings and future retirement income will be affected negatively."[26]

"For the overwhelming majority of retirement savers," according to the University of Michigan report, "there is no evidence of portfolio rebalancing, shifts in risk tolerance with age, or tactical portfolio changes."[27]

Work with a Financial Professional

A number of financial professionals can help you negotiate Wall Street far better than you could on your own. They include stockbrokers, certified public accountants (CPAs), attorneys (J.D.s), registered investment advisers (RIAs), and Certified Financial Planners™ (CFPs®). An important distinction can be made between the stockbrokers and the remaining four professionals.

Under federal law, stockbrokers who sell securities to the public are held to a "suitability" standard. In other words, they are required to sell products that are suitable for the buyer's situation or goals. RIAs and CFPs®, in contrast, are required by law to adhere to a higher standard known as a "fiduciary" standard. The word derives from the Latin *fides*, meaning "trust." Those operating under a fiduciary standard must recommend products that are not only "suitable" but also "in the best interests of" the client. CPAs and attorneys may owe the client a fiduciary duty, but may not.[28]

Suppose a client was investing $10,000 a year for retirement. A financial professional could ethically recommend a product that earns 6 percent (and make a nice profit for herself and her company) and solidly meet the "suitability" criterion required by law. That investment would grow to $800,000 in 30 years. A fiduciary, however, would be obligated to inform the client of another investment that earns 8.5 percent. After 30 years, a client using this investment would see his or her nest egg grow to $1.1 million, a $300,000 difference.

It is important to note that many stockbrokers are in fact also CFPs® or investment adviser representatives of RIAs. As such, they must conform to the fiduciary standard.[29]

Who Is a Fiduciary?

The financial professionals with a legal requirement to operate as a fiduciary include accountants, attorneys, registered investment advisers, and Certified Financial Planners. Among these, the CFP® is the designation that is most closely aligned with financial planning (no surprise).

CFPs® are required to pass an exhaustive and difficult 11-hour exam, which requires several years of training. Regular, continuing education is also required. A CFP® has the ability and obligation to get to know you and your financial situation. When you contact a CFP®, he or she must interview you at length to learn your plans and goals. The CFP® can then provide advice based on your very personal, individual financial situation. A CFP® will eventually prepare for you an individualized, strategic plan. Certified Financial Planners™ can easily be found in the phone book or on the Internet at http://www.cfp.net.

Is your adviser certified? While it is strongly recommended that you fully explore the possible benefits of retaining a professional with a fiduciary standard, most financial representatives of all stripes are solid, ethical professionals. Liz Pulliam Weston in *MSN Money* suggests that you ask your financial professional the following questions:

- Are you legally obligated to act in my best interests at all times? (She encourages clients to ask for this promise in writing.)
- Will you disclose all potential conflicts of interest? (In other words, does the selling of a certain product help the professional's compensation in some significant way?)
- In what ways are you compensated? (You may prefer an adviser who works on a flat-fee basis rather than gaining a commission for every product sold.)[30]

Using a professional is far preferable to dealing with Wall Street on your own. And as a last point, in general, it just doesn't make sense to get your investment tips from your neighbor over the backyard fence. Contact a professional.

STRATEGY #4 Checklist

☑ Do not take on Wall Street alone; employ a licensed financial professional.

☑ Employ a licensed financial professional who is a fiduciary and has the legal requirement to act in your best interest.

☑ To start, search sites such as the CFP® Board's website (http://www.cfp.net).

Maintain Your Own Personal Bailout Fund

THE MISCONCEPTION: GOVERNMENT BAILOUTS ARE FOR THE INSIDERS, NOT THE PEOPLE

September 2008 started an amazing trend in America. Washington, D.C., simply handed over cold cash, by the hundreds of billions of dollars, directly to private corporations. These actions went by various names: the bailouts, TARP, rescuing AIG. These infusions of cash have been handy for greedy insiders, but you and I, the public, will never receive a bailout from the U.S. government.

Weaving a Gold(man) Web

The story starts with Goldman Sachs, of course. After contributing heavily to the housing bubble by securitizing hundreds of billions in subprime mortgages, Goldman realized how shaky these investments were. In the likely scenario that millions of mortgage holders became unable to make their monthly payments, the investment bank wanted to make sure it still had a way to make a profit. Goldman's bankers turned to their buddies on Wall Street, American International Group (AIG), the largest insurer in the world. As we learned in Strategy #4, Goldman exploited a unique product to disguise subprime mortgages, the collateralized debt obligation (CDO). AIG then provided for Goldman its own version of a unique three-initialed product to insure it: the CDS (credit default swap).[1]

The name and initials are irrelevant, except for the purpose of confusing the average American and hiding fraud behind sophisticated verbiage. What you need to know is that AIG had almost no reserves to back up its promise to bail out hundreds of billions in mortgages securitized or sold by Goldman Sachs.

Imagine this situation in a different industry. It would be difficult for life insurance companies like Prudential or Northwestern to pocket monthly premiums, since they must have billions' worth of reserves to show government regulators in case their customers do, in fact, die. But somehow the world's largest insurer, AIG, got away with failing to follow a rather obviously necessary regulation that requires money in the bank to back up a bailout promise.

In 2008, rating agencies like Moody's and Standard & Poor's finally uncovered the fact that the government had failed to regulate an insurer. Hundreds of billions of worthless mortgages were failing, and no insurance existed to stop the bleeding.

Of course, the biggest bleeder should have been Goldman Sachs, but instead of this company reaping the consequences of bad business decisions, a massive full-court press was carried out by banking industry lobbyists to convince Americans that the bleeding victim was actually the entire U.S. economy. If something were not done immediately, the entire financial system would implode. Riots, martial law, and chaos unimaginable would ensue unless the U.S. government handed over hundreds of billions, if not trillions, of dollars to the nation's largest banks.

Goldman's Financial Fraternity

Leading this charge was U.S. Secretary of the Treasury Henry (Hank) Paulson. Before President George W. Bush appointed him to oversee the U.S. Treasury in 2004, Paulson was the CEO of Goldman. This key bit of information might help explain why Paulson and the head of AIG and Goldman held an emergency meeting in New York when the market crashed: AIG was about to go bankrupt, and it owed Goldman $13 billion in CDS contracts.[2]

The result of the meeting was that AIG received an $85 billion bailout from the federal government to prevent the collapse of civilization, or so the hype went. So Goldman Sachs received its $13 billion in insurance from AIG, for issuing bonds backed by subprime loans. That same day, Hank Paulson hopped back and forth from another meeting in New York involving Lehman Brothers. Lehman was also hemorrhaging. However, the investment bank had the unfortunate status of being Goldman Sachs's number one competitor, and Lehman, for reasons still not articulated, was left to die. No bailout for you!

As President Obama's chief of staff Rahm Emanuel stated in November 2009, "You never want a serious crisis to go to waste."[3] And Treasury Secretary Paulson wasted no time in selling a $700 billion bailout extravaganza called the Troubled Asset Relief Program (TARP) to the president and Congress. To oversee the money, Paulson appointed a 35-year-old ex-Goldman banker named Neel Kashkari. Goldman helped itself to $10 billion of these TARP funds and then switched itself from an investment bank to a bank holding company in order to receive more money—perhaps hundreds of billions—from the Federal Reserve. Conveniently, the organization's new status as a holding company left Goldman to be supervised by the New York Fed itself, whose chairman, Stephen Friedman, was (drum roll here) the ex-chairman of Goldman!

This new arrangement caused a couple of problems. First, Friedman was still on the board of Goldman but was now also regulating the company. Second, he owned millions in Goldman stock. To solve the problem, he requested a waiver from the federal government to regulate a bank on whose board he still served and to own substantial amounts of stock in a bank whose future he could help shape . . . and he got a letter of permission for both.

He then went and bought 52,000 *additional* shares of Goldman stock, putting himself in a position to earn millions more from any growth in Goldman Sachs.[4]

Commit a Crime, Get a Bonus

Now, the folks over at AIG—the ones who had made billions collecting insurance premiums with no reserves—made out quite well. AIG's Financial Products unit, the 400-employee subdivision that handled the insuring of subprimes, increased its revenues 434 percent, from $737 million in 1999 to $3.2 billion in 2005. Those 400 employees received $3.5 billion in compensation over roughly the same time period. The head of the group, Joe Cassano, earned $280 million.[5]

In 2007, when the ratings agencies were blowing the whistle, Cassano held a conference call with AIG's investors, operators of funds that handle Granny's small nest egg. He knew AIG's portfolio had already lost $352 million, but instead of admitting the loss, Cassano appears to have been particularly brazen, telling the group of conference callers, "It is hard for us, and without being flippant, to even see a scenario within any kind of realm of reason that would see us losing $1 in any of those transactions."[6]

A few months later, AIG announced $11.5 billion in losses.

Was Cassano arrested? No, he wasn't convicted of any crime. In fact, he really wasn't even fired. He was relieved of his executive status but was allowed to keep $34 million in bonuses. He also remained with the company as a consultant and was paid $1 million a month for several months, including after AIG received the $85 billion bailout caused by Cassano and his team's hubris that led them to take enormous bets with taxpayer money. When asked by Congress about this, new AIG CEO Martin Sullivan said the $1 million monthly fee was still being paid "to retain the 20-year knowledge that Mr. Cassano had."[7]

In January 2009, AIG decided to reward all of Cassano's 400 employees as well. They each received an average of $1.1 million in total compensation, totaling $450 million. Why? "To keep these highly expert people in their seats," said AIG spokesperson Christina Pretto.[8]

Not too much later, the new treasury secretary under President Obama, Timothy Geithner, announced another $30 billion bailout for AIG. This one left the cable news networks scratching their heads, but only a little bit of digging was needed: Geithner, a disciple of Goldman executive John Thain, was a key player in Paulson's earlier bailouts of Goldman and AIG. Geithner picked as his chief of staff former Goldman Sachs lobbyist Mark Patterson. And Obama replaced Neel Kashkari, the Goldmanite picked by Hank Paulson to oversee the $700 billion in TARP funds, with former co-finance chief of Goldman Sachs, Gary Gensler. During those tough electioneering days when funds are critical to success, Barack Obama's top private donor had been, yes, Goldman Sachs.[9]

Global Warming: Big, Hot Bucks

Investigative reporter Matt Taibbi says the next bubble Goldman Sachs expects to inflate will be bigger than all the rest: the infamous cap-and-trade initiative to reduce greenhouse gases will create "carbon credits" that will be heavily regulated by Obama's Goldman Sachs appointees. They will be traded on the Chicago Climate Exchange, 10 percent of which is currently owned by Goldman Sachs. Al Gore, a key player in the cap-and-trade bill being pushed by the Obama administration, has started up a company called Generation Investment Management that plans to take advantage of the billion- to trillion-dollar carbon credit market. Three former Goldman execs are also owners with Gore.

Terms like "cap and trade" and "carbon credits" can be difficult to understand. Matt Taibbi says the Wall Street insiders like it that way:

> There is a reason it used to be a crime in the Confederate states to teach a slave to read. Literacy is power. . . . In the age of CDS and CDO, most of us are financial illiterates. By making the already too-complex economy even more complex, Wall Street

has used the crisis to effect a historic, revolutionary change in our political system. . . . The worldwide economic meltdown and the bailout that followed . . . cemented and formalized a political trend that has been snowballing for decades: the gradual take-over of the government by a small class of connected insiders, who used money to control elections, buy influence, and systematically weaken regulations.[10]

So in this day when the average guy is struggling to make it but the giant corporations are getting massive amounts of financial assistance, just remember this: the government is never going to bail you out.

THE TRUTH: THE INSIDERS SAVED US FROM TOTAL COLLAPSE

The last sentence you just read about the bailout misconception ("The government is never going to bail you out") is both true and false. It is true that none of us regular folk in the flyover zone will ever have massive amounts of cash sent our way to shore up the holes in our bad investments or to rescue us from the inevitable calamities in life. That is why it is so important for each of us to create our own bailout fund, something we will discuss in detail in the strategy section of this chapter.

It is false to think, however, that there is no circumstance in which individuals can get a personal bailout; it happens all the time. In fact, it is quite similar to what happened to these Wall Street firms with TARP and the other bailout events. This phenomenon is known as bankruptcy.

Like some of the corporate outrages detailed in the bailout misconception, a person who declares bankruptcy often watches his or her thousands in credit card and other debt—maybe as much as $50,000 or even $100,000—simply vanish with no requirement to repay it ever again. Bankruptcy, however, should always be avoided. Bankruptcy intrudes on your life, requiring you to reveal your personal and financial details to complete strangers: 180 days before filing for bankruptcy, a person who wishes to file must seek credit counseling from a government-approved organization at his or her own expense.[11] The next humiliating step is to explain to a bankruptcy judge, in open court, exactly how your financial affairs became unmanageable. The court's records are public and often appear in the newspaper.

Filing for bankruptcy will also affect your credit score (remaining on your credit report for at least seven years) and may prevent you from getting a job, home loan (or even renting a house if a credit check is required), car loan, life insurance, and credit cards.[12] In addition, bankruptcy is expensive. On top of the cost of credit counseling, petitioners must pay for debtor education, lawyers, filings fees, and any debt not discharged, such as student loans or back taxes.[13]

The pain of personal bankruptcy is somewhat similar to what happened with the U.S. government's bailout of firms like AIG, Merrill Lynch, and Bear Stearns. Government regulators moved in and told them how to proceed with their business. Further irresponsible lending and asset acquisition were prohibited. The public became aware of their poor management. Yes, they received relief from their toxic (terrible) assets, but just as in an individual bankruptcy, these companies were forced to face the music of severe restrictions.

Unlike the popular misconception, the executives for many of these firms *were* fired across the board, including senior officials at Merrill Lynch and Bear Stearns. All the AIG executives dealing with credit default swaps, and ultimately Cassano, were let go. People say, "These rich guys were bailed out!" but actually, most of these rich guys lost their jobs and the majority of their wealth because it was tied up in their company. They were also embarrassed over the whole ordeal. None of these guys were rehired in the financial services market. There were some cases where inappropriate actions occurred, such as the bonuses received by the AIG employees, but the vast majority of the bailout plan was successful.

When you consider the actions of U.S. Treasury Secretary Henry Paulson as "forcing bankruptcy on Wall Street firms," it doesn't sound nearly as irresponsible, or suspicious, as a "bailout."

Shouldn't We Just Let the Whole Thing Collapse?

Before we get to the specifics of what the Treasury did in terms of regulating these companies, let's talk about the reason it was imperative for the Treasury to intervene during the financial crisis. Many might ask, "Why not just let AIG fail? Why not let the market take its natural course and ultimately correct itself?" The answer is that many of the men of the hour—Paulson, Fed chairman Ben Bernanke, and others—feared, and rightly so, that the failure of AIG would lead to a run on the banks, in which many customers withdraw all of their funds in fear of the bank being insolvent.[14]

Most of us saw the movie *It's a Wonderful Life* when we were kids. If you remember, Jimmy Stewart was devastated when the clerks of the bank he owned were forced to tell a growing and angry crowd that they had run out of money.

Early in life, we think the bank just puts our money in the vault and leaves it there until the day comes that we ask for it back. As we grow up, we learn that the process is a bit more complex. The bank takes our money, lends it to others for a fee, and makes a profit both for them and for us.

Now, you might think it is risky for a bank not to have all the money available for all its customers all the time. Centuries of experience, however, have shown that rarely, if ever, do all the customers demand their money out of the vaults simultaneously. Over the years, a somewhat exact formula has evolved as to what percentage of money a bank ought to have in its vaults at any particular time to meet the needs of customers who do want their money back in their pockets immediately. (As of 2011, that number is around 10 percent.[15])

Let's say your local small-town bank—let's call it the Bank of Mayberry—has 10 customers, and each of these customers has $1,000 in the bank. The bank would therefore have $10,000 in its vault and should be able to repay all the customers if they all asked for it at the same time. But the reality is that the bank has also made loans far exceeding the $10,000 deposited by those 10 customers.

Even if all the customers of the Bank of Mayberry demanded their money, however, they would still be able to receive it. Why? Because of the "FDIC Insured" sign you see on the wall of nearly every bank in the country. The Federal Deposit Insurance Corporation exists for the very purpose of preventing a run on the banks. Anything up to $250,000 is insured. If the Bank of Mayberry can't pay you today, the FDIC will make sure you get your money a couple of days later.

How an AIG Failure Might Have Started a Bank Run

Ordinarily, the idea of a run on the bank is not a problem. But it became a serious issue in September 2008, when Treasury Secretary Paulson realized that AIG could fail. If the company did so, it would cause a number of the largest banks in the country to fail as well. For example, Citigroup was scheduled to lose $9 billion because of AIG's inability to insure some of the bad loans on Citibank's books. Such a gigantic loss would have forced Citibank to declare bankruptcy at its next reporting period at the end of the month. What would Citibank's customers do? They would demand their money. Citibank would not have it, and the FDIC would have to bail *everyone* out.

Bank of America might have made a similar announcement. But JPMorgan might not have had any problem, and it could assure its customers that all was well. Unfortunately, by this time, the public would be terrified, due to the potential bankruptcy of Bank of America and Citibank, so it would be likely that customers would also demand their money from JPMorgan. As discussed before, JPMorgan would have only 10 percent or less of its obligations handy, so it, too, would be forced to rely on the FDIC.

A run on the banks at this high of a level would have created a massive crisis in America. Even if the FDIC had enough billions and trillions to bail out everyone (and this is doubtful), it certainly would have been far less expensive to bail out the company that started the problem: AIG. This is exactly what Paulson and company chose to do.

We may never learn the whole story behind the bailout, but often five or ten years after such situations, personal accounts of senior government officials' actions are revealed, such as why Lehman Brothers was allowed to fail but AIG was rescued. Perhaps the leaders may even admit that the AIG bailout occurred due to fear of a run on the banks. A year after the bailout crisis, Treasury Secretary Timothy Geithner admitted to such a giant fear. "By September 2008, for the first time in 80 years," he testified, "the United States risked a complete collapse of our financial system."[16]

Former New York insurance regulator Eric Dinallo, who did not oversee AIG and had no interest in bailing out AIG's bad paper, admitted that the bailout "may not have been handled perfectly, but we believed then that we were staring into the abyss." The crisis would not have destroyed the institutions only, said Dinallo, it would have dried up financing for every small business in America, forcing them to shut down and let go of their employees. "The point is that there is no business or individual who would not have been hurt by such a collapse and who did not benefit from avoiding it," he said.[17]

While some might have liked to see everything collapse and rebuild from scratch, such massive change is not the job of elected officials. Their job is not to allow chaos to ensue but rather to promote a stable society. Fed Chairman Ben Bernanke, in the opinion of many, was also the right man at the right time for the job. He is well known in the academic community as an expert on the Great Depression and even wrote his doctoral dissertation on the topic and how to avoid another one in the future. If there was a person to have in the inner circle at the time of the crisis, he was the one.

Other high-level investment advisers are also complimentary of Bernanke's actions as chairman of the Federal Reserve from January 2006 to the present. Noting that the Fed increased its lending by 32 times in 2009—a radical innovation—it is neverthe-less the case that all non-Fed lending dramatically decreased. The Fed's increased activity made up for only one-sixth of the nation-wide drop in lending.[18]

Expect a Giant Squid to Be Ubiquitous

Now what about the perception that so many players in the bail-out game were associated with Goldman Sachs?

The first thing to note is that Goldman Sachs is the key player, the most revered and sought-out company in the financial indus-try. Many executives there make enough money to retire early and look for a way to contribute in government service, and it should therefore be expected that Goldman Sachs alumni are found serv-ing in various sectors of the public and the economy.

Noting that Goldman Sachs alumni are everywhere in the economy would be like saying Ivy Leaguers dominate the cor-porate landscape with CEOs. That is why freelance writer Matt Taibbi, in his well-read article in *Rolling Stone*, referred to Gold-man Sachs as a "giant vampire squid." They are indeed a force to be reckoned with, ubiquitous on the economic landscape. Fur-thermore, pointing out that many key players are associated with Goldman Sachs is like complaining that most NFL coaches are in some way associated with the Cowboys or the Steelers. Well, that's because they were the best teams in the NFL for several decades.

Take, for example, Stephen Friedman, the head of the New York Fed when Goldman Sachs switched from being an invest-ment bank to a commercial bank holding company. Friedman, who became chairman of the New York Fed nine months earlier, had no idea this transfer would occur. When it did take place, he realized his equity ownership in the firm and his then-current board of directors position at the firm might create a conflict in now regulating them, and offered to resign.

Instead of accepting Friedman's resignation, the New York Federal Reserve Bank's board of directors gave him a waiver to remain on for a few months. He told the board he would not divest himself of stock, but the board said that was allowable, for a few months.[19] This situation was not the best of scenarios, but also not necessarily criminal. It was based on extenuating circumstances during an unprecedented series of events. Friedman did, in fact, resign in a few months, and those conflicts are no longer an issue.[20]

It should also be noted that most of the bailout was not for Goldman Sachs, but for other banks. Goldman did get $10 billion of the TARP money, true. But the government guaranteed *$306 billion* of Citigroup's assets. They also guaranteed *$118 billion* in assets for Bank of America. So if there was a major "bailout," it was for those two banks, not Goldman Sachs. Also, banks were not the only organizations getting bailout money from the federal government. Nearly $30 billion went to General Motors, Chrysler, and other automobile-related companies.

Not All, but Most of the Motivations Were Good Ones

Now, there may be some truth to the charge that Goldman insiders were motivated to let their competitor Lehman Brothers fail. Leaders at the senior level on Wall Street are as competitive, and as extraordinarily strong in personality, as an athlete for the Yankees or the Lakers. As in any situation where you have several high-ego players in the same room, the best you can hope for is that they coexist peacefully.

Dick Fuld, the head of Lehman Brothers, was one of those strong personalities. And at the end of the day, Hank Paulson was still the head of the U.S. Treasury, and Dick Fuld was out of a job. We'll never know all the motivations involved. However, it appears that most of the decisions made during the critical bailout period were for the best interests of the U.S. economy.

In fact, cold cash was not simply handed to these bailed-out companies. The transaction was a bit more complicated than that. The government did not hand over cash, but instead bought or guaranteed some of the toxic assets owned by these financial institutions. There is good reason to believe that by 2020 or so, many of these assets, a large portion of which are based on real estate, will be worth far more than the paltry amount the market is willing to pay for them in 2011.

And not only does the government have the possibility of being paid back if these assets return to their earlier value, the government required all these banks to issue warrants (or call options, which allow the owner to profit when the underlying security rises in price) to the federal government, meaning that if the assets recover and do well over time, the government could actually make a profit from them.

The case can be made that Henry Paulson, Ben Bernanke, Timothy Geithner, and others had good reason to take drastic action in September 2008 to keep the economy afloat. Specific moves taken did not simply involve fistfuls of cash being handed to cronies, but instead calculated purchases of strategic assets that could possibly bring a profit back to the government over time. And while Goldman Sachs alumni do in fact dot the landscape of the financial world, that fact in itself does not prove conspiracy. It just proves that Goldman hires the best and the brightest, and these people tend to move to the highest levels of the corporate and political world.

So we once again return to the question asked in the previous chapter: Who is at fault for the crisis of 2008? Is no one to blame? In addition to the declining standards of the American consumer, as discussed, perhaps the root problem was the government's failure to regulate the bad business decisions of Wall Street over the past two decades. However, while increased regulation may or may not help, regulation alone will not solve an unlikely systemic risk.

While it's not the purpose of the book to solve economic issues and prevent future financial meltdowns, the blame game played by the media and politicians often obscures an important question: What actions should be taken or implemented in the short term to prevent the catastrophe that just occurred from being repeated? Perhaps an insurance model would be more effective in combating this potential issue in the future. If someone chooses to make a high-risk investment, that investor should be required to pay for insurance on the investment in case it fails. For example, the Federal Reserve, U.S. Treasury, and other government agencies provided zero- or low-cost loans, guaranteed assets, or took over various financial and industrial institutions to prevent a systemic failure. Many government officials used the phrase "too big to fail" and argued that if any of those institutions (e.g., Citigroup, Goldman, AIG) failed, then the entire system would collapse. So if the government is effectively insuring all these institutions from total failure, shouldn't those institutions be paying an "insurance premium" for that coverage?

Does the government require you and me to pay for insurance if we drive a car? Yes, and with good reason. Certain accidents could end up costing far more than we could ever pay. Insurance prevents financial debacles from occurring, for both individuals and corporations.

In the past 20 years, financial institutions found a way to squirm around regulations requiring a certain percentage of reserves while lending billions of dollars, or were able to avoid purchasing insurance on iffy mortgages. Goldman Sachs, even though not required to have insurance, sought out AIG to insure its iffy subprime mortgages. And rightly so. AIG, however, found a way to promise insurance to Goldman without being required to own the necessary reserves. Had this been required, the bailout might never have been necessary.

THE STRATEGY: MAINTAIN YOUR OWN PERSONAL BAILOUT FUND

Everyone has times in life when the unexpected jumps in front of our best-laid plans. From job loss to illness to family issues to rainy days, having six months' worth of cash in the bank allows you to weather these storms without derailing your financial future. (Remember our 20–7–6 formula?) What happened in September 2008 is interesting. It does affect you to a degree, but it has very little effect on you compared with the decisions you will make regarding your own portfolio.

You cannot control much of the macro economy. However, you can control your own micro economy. While a bailout in 2008 may have saved the national economy from collapse, the federal government will not be there for you if you have a personal financial crisis. You need to create a fund for yourself—your own personal bailout fund—to rescue your retirement plan if things go awry for a few months.

Your Personal Bailout Fund

Your bailout fund starts with a minimum of six months of spending money "in the bank" through various securities like money market funds or bank savings accounts. That's step number one to bail yourself out. And in a recession, a nine-month bailout fund is an even better idea.

There are three important reasons to save enough for an emergency bailout fund:

1. **It takes a long time to find a job.** A 2010 news article highlighted the phenomenon of "severance societies": the people who were laid off in 2007 or 2008 with severance started running out of money three to four years later. They never changed their lifestyle. If they made $150,000, they got $150,000 in severance. They received one year's salary, they had some savings, and a year later they still didn't have a job, but they acted as if they had a ton of money. They should have been storing up six to nine months' worth of pay for their bailout fund.

   It takes a long time to find a job, and there are systemically unemployed people who just can't seem to do it. Others refuse to take a job below their station, so if they were making $100,000 before, are they going to take a job for $75,000? "No," they say, "I'm going to hold out until I get a job for $100,000 or higher." Well, OK, but that is *insane*. A reasonable person takes a job for $75,000 to stop his or her financial bleeding and hopes to see that salary increase over the years.

2. **You can avoid being wiped out by medical expenses.** Health care expenses can wipe you out before you have time to blink. If you do not have a considerable cushion of savings, even if you do not lose your job, if you or someone in your family has a severe medical condition that cannot be completely covered by insurance, then you need to have a lot of savings on hand. To this point, a recent study by Harvard found that *62 percent* of bankruptcies in 2007 in the United States were caused by medical expenses.[21] Let's face it, it would be wonderful to retire someday, but if you go bankrupt and can't pay your medical bills today, next week, or next year, it does not matter whether or not you built a retirement portfolio.

3. **You can avoid credit card debt.** A large portion of America lives paycheck to paycheck, which not only makes it extremely difficult to save for retirement, but also creates an incredible stress when an unforeseen bill hits you. Let's think about the possible situations: What if you lose your job temporarily? What if you have a medical issue? What if someone in your family needs to borrow money? What if your washer or dryer breaks? What if your car engine blows? What if you get a leak in your roof? What if you are hit with any of those relatively expensive maintenance issues that we all deal with from time to time, and you don't have any savings?

Of course, you have a problem if you have to live with a leaky roof. You have an arguably worse problem if you have to go into debt—credit card debt—in order to pay for that roof. Quite frankly, if you live paycheck to paycheck and use your credit card for unusual expenses, *chances are you will never get out of credit card debt*. You are stuck. So reason number three ultimately means this: you need a six-month bailout fund so you never need to use your credit card and see that debt spiral into your financial ruin.

Getting a Home Equity Loan Likely Will Not Work

Some people may think a separate cash fund is unnecessary. Can't you always get a home equity loan, or even cash out a mutual fund or some other asset in your IRA or 401(k)?

Those are terrible ideas. It is incredibly difficult to get a home equity loan at a time of financial stress, such as when you have just lost your job. By counting on a home equity loan, you are making two main assumptions:

1. **Your credit is good, and a bank will give you a home equity loan.** Remember, you are only pursuing this option if you are already experiencing a financial problem. Otherwise, you live paycheck to paycheck. For an example, suppose your friend Jim has lost his job. If he tries to get a home equity loan and the banker says to him, "Where are you currently employed?" he would say, "Well, I've lost my job." That's a much different conversation than before he lost his job. This is not a criticism; bankers are trying to be repaid. And the number one criterion for paying off a loan, or paying the monthly rent, is that you have a job.
2. **The bank's appraisal will value your house for more than you owe on your current mortgage.** The market has been cruel to housing prices lately. Home values are down by 50 percent in parts of Florida, Nevada, and California. So, if you had a 20 percent cushion and your house price goes down by 50 percent, when you go in for your home equity loan, guess what? You are underwater. You are not going to get anything.

Mutual Funds May Not Help You Either

What about mutual funds? Consider when people are losing their jobs. Are they being let go when the Dow is at 14,000 and their mutual fund is worth more than they paid for it? Or are they losing their jobs when the Dow is at 8,000 and 9,000 and 5,000 and 7,000, and their mutual fund is worth a lot less than what they paid for it? Clearly, it is the latter.

So yes, if you have a mutual fund and you put $10,000 into it, come crisis time, it is now worth $7,000. Sure, you still have $7,000. But even then, it takes a while to get that money. You can make the call to have it mailed to you, but now you are looking at three to five days until you receive the check and maybe another two or three days before such a large deposit clears your bank. That is a large risk to take with your emergency fund. To be clear, an emergency fund is cash that should be available to you *within a day*. You could also think of it like funding a three-day vacation, and you decide you need the money on a Friday afternoon and the bank's not open again until Monday—but cash you can touch within three days.

Is the mutual fund in your IRA or 401(k)? If you sell and withdraw cash from a retirement account (tax deferred), you will get hit with a penalty of 10 percent *plus* your tax rate. And the wait will be much longer than five to ten days, because now you have to go apply—in the case of a 401(k), to your company's human resources department—to request an early withdrawal. Yes, they will most likely grant it. The penalty makes no difference to them, since you are the one who gets taxed on it. But it is still a serious process, and the bigger the company, the longer it takes. It may take you a month to get the cash.

When you cash out mutual funds and retirement assets, you are not only incurring enormous tax penalties, but also probably selling at the lowest possible price. The crisis you are in is likely precipitated by a larger national financial crisis, meaning your mutual fund is worth a lot less than you paid for it. But you are also admitting to your company that you have a big, big problem. Do you want to do that? Maybe you're comfortable with this, but probably not. Wouldn't it be a lot easier just to have cash squirreled away?

Bankruptcy Is a Nightmare: Saving for Six Months Is Much Easier

Earlier, we discussed that the government does in fact have a bailout plan for individuals as well as Wall Street corporations. Yes, you can be bailed out if necessary, but you really don't want to file for personal bankruptcy.

These days, it is incredibly difficult to go through bankruptcy. The George W. Bush administration changed laws to make it much harder to file for bankruptcy (perhaps that was actually good). Mostly, banks favored the change in the laws because a lot of people were getting into incredible credit card debt, and then they would say, "Yep. I'm bankrupt. I don't have enough." And the courts would wipe the slate clean.

And guess what those people would go do? They would find another credit card once their credit went up slightly. Bankruptcy did not interrupt their lives. It did not stop their jobs, nor did it stop their spending plans, because the bankruptcy court cannot take your wages. So banks really lost out, and it was a moral hazard for the individual.

Now it is much more difficult to get those debts wiped clean. Plus, you incur enormous expenses because you likely have to be represented by an attorney to go through the whole process. And at the end, you have bankruptcy on your credit report, which means no one is going to want to lend you any money for seven years. Your employer is going to know about it, and you will likely suffer considerable personal embarrassment. This all assumes you can get through the bankruptcy process without being left with onerous debt payments.

So bail yourself out proactively. Don't wait until the world ends and say, "Oh! I don't know what to do." Wouldn't it be easier to save a little every month until you've saved six months' worth of cash, so when you hit one of these problems, it's not the end of the world for you?

Arm yourself with an emergency bailout fund.

STRATEGY #5 Checklist

☑ Create a personal bailout fund of at least six months' spending money in money market funds or bank savings accounts.

☑ Do not count on home equity loans or a disbursement from your retirement account as your bailout, as this can take valuable time when an emergency occurs.

Rather than Accruing Debt, Accumulate Savings

THE MISCONCEPTION: LEVERAGE IS THE KEY TO PROSPERITY

Average Americans may do well to avoid any kind of debt or leverage during their lives—that is, if they simply want to remain average. For those looking to become prosperous, leveraging their money is the key to success.

The Money Matador writes a blog (at http://www.moneymata dor.com) that names credit card debt as a way to borrow to prosperity. The blog's tagline, "Entrepreneurship, get rich, and a bit of fun," meshes well with the Matador's advice to use credit cards to buy items on eBay or obtain early low-cost airline tickets and sell them later for a profit. If the profit exceeds the interest on the cards, then you are in business![1]

Real estate investor Carleton Sheets has made millions upon millions encouraging people to commence the beginning of future fortunes by buying real estate properties with no money down. "Using creative financing techniques is an art that most real estate investors fail to master," Sheets explains. "Using the proper creative financing techniques at the right time is critical to your real estate investing success."[2]

Kevin Jarrett in Cape Coral, Florida, used Other People's Money (the bank) to get rich quickly. A mental health counselor, he put only $1,000 down on a house and then watched the equity grow. Three years later, he was able to quit his job and sell real estate full-time. He began renting out homes, borrowing against their rising equity, and continuing to increase his nest egg, using the age-old trick of leverage. Kevin's life upgraded to $100 dinners, a powerboat, and a yellow Corvette (which he included in the photo for his business card).[3]

"The more leverage the better," says Internet trading adviser Adam Milton. He explains that making a $300 profit off investing $3,000 in the market is no comparison to making $1,000 instead with the same money. How? By getting a $7,000 loan to make the investment $10,000 instead of $3,000—"buying on margin," as it is called in the investment world. "Professional traders will choose highly leveraged markets over non-leveraged markets every time," writes Milton on About.com. "Telling new traders to avoid trading using leverage is essentially telling them to trade like an amateur instead of a professional."[4]

The Blixseths

Consider the lives of Tim and Edra Blixseth, who took enormous risks and racked up millions in debt along their way to the Fortune 400. In the 1990s, their successes allowed them to build a 13,600-acre private ski resort in Montana, boasting the most elite members in the world, including billionaires such as Bill Gates.[5] A decade earlier, in 1986, the Blixseths had found themselves with $15.4 million in debt and only $4,400 in assets. No problem. They simply filed bankruptcy, and Tim Blixseth searched for more opportunities, using borrowed money to make high-level deals in the timber industry to amass yet another fortune. In one of those timber deals, he acquired a massive tract of land in the wilds of Montana and used it to develop the world's most exclusive ski resort.

The Blixseths built themselves a 30,000-square-foot home to go along with a 240-acre private golf course, a pool guarded by bronze lions, and a 1,700-foot driveway. A gym, beauty parlor, private theater, massage alcoves, and Buddhist prayer room can all be found inside the house. One room is filled with furniture from the 18th century, while the bedroom has pieces from the Vatican.

Their private ski resort, named Yellowstone after the national park in Montana, provides 75 ski runs with names like "Learjet Glades." Tim and Edra installed a caviar bar in the clubhouse. But the main reason folks such as the CEO of Comcast, the world's top investment bankers, golf superstar Annika Sörenstam, and the owner of the Los Angeles Dodgers joined Gates as members is the club's privacy and exclusive aspect. Particularly for Gates, he likes the fact that his kids don't have to be constantly followed around by bodyguards. At Vail, all the security "made us look like jerks," he said. "Here, we don't need it."

"Private Powder" was an early slogan for the Yellowstone ski resort. Later, the motto changed to "Where families gather." To gather, these members initially had to pay $250,000 to join. They also were required to buy a $5 million to $35 million home on the development property.

All this success and prosperity did not frighten the Blixseths into sticking with what they had and staying put financially. Rather, they continued working the same formula of using other people's money, or debt, to build even greater successes. The Blixseths earned a spot on the Forbes 400 list with over $1 billion in net worth. When they needed more cash for their broader ambitions of building a chain of Yellowstone Clubs across the world, Credit Suisse loaned them $375 million. Over time, the couple purchased various exotic properties such as a castle outside Paris for $28 million, a Caribbean island for another $28 million, and a $40 million golf retreat in Scotland.

For Tim and Edra Blixseth, borrowing money and taking on enormous debt seems to have worked out pretty well. While a lot of straitlaced folks out there will constantly remind you to stay out of debt, remember it is those who take the risk of debt who enjoy the reward of prosperity.

THE TRUTH: LEVERAGE IS DEBT—AND IS ALMOST ALWAYS A BAD IDEA

Leading authorities believe that debt causes harm in many ways. A Dun & Bradstreet study showed that credit card users spend 12 to 18 percent more when purchasing goods and services with plastic instead of cash. The reason: swiping a plastic card doesn't seem to hurt as much as handing over actual paper money.[6] In addition, finances are listed as the leading cause of divorce by a factor of four to one over any other cause, including infidelity—a significant problem, considering that approximately 50 percent of all marriages fail.

The story of Tim and Edra Blixseth certainly has a short-term sound of success. They took on millions in debt, nearly a billion dollars, and have lived in the lap of luxury. At least that was the case until 2007.

According to Edra Blixseth, the $375 million loan from Credit Suisse in 2005 was "the beginning of the end of my personal and business relationship with Tim." Edra has filed for bankruptcy. Their divorce is pending. Certain court documents show her holding nearly a billion dollars in debts. A judge ordered her arrest for failing to appear in court over only one of her many multimillion-dollar loans that have gone unpaid. Foreclosure on her 30,000-square-foot home looms over her.

Once the king of the hill, her husband is now despised by many of the Yellowstone Club members, and not just because he left the resort in financial straits: sewage backed up at the ski lodge, potholes went unrepaired, and the power grid regularly failed to operate for the 300 homes at the development.

Edra now thinks even less of her former husband. To press the point with friends, at a recent party she held (which cost $90,000), the decor included specially made piñatas resembling her husband—a kind of voodoo doll filled with chocolate gold coins that spilled out when the piñatas were struck with a big stick.

For his part, Tim has refused to talk to reporters about his financial woes and has simply continued with the plan that has always worked for him, creating bigger visions and getting borrowed money to finance them—except this time, it may not be working so well. He made headlines in 2006 with the announcement that he would build the most expensive home in the world. Priced at $155 million, this 53,000-square-foot home known as Pinnacle was slated to include a heliport, an ice-skating rink, and an underground parking lot for 20 SUVs. Only the driveway was built, however. He sold the lot.[7]

Kevin Jarrett, the mental health counselor turned real estate mogul, also has a "rest of the story" about his journey toward quick riches. As profiled in a *New York Times* piece on real estate bubbles bursting, Jarrett found himself holding the bag. His monthly income plummeted to $4,200 after the bubble burst, and he expected it to drop further as real estate is not selling; his rental properties provided another $3,500, but he owed his lenders $17,000 a month. He's selling a nutritional juice now and looking for state-subsidized health care for his family. He expects to sell all his properties and start over. "I'm in survival mode," he told the *Times*.[8]

Buying on margin—basically, borrowing money to buy securities—may be one of the strongest examples of how to lose money quickly through the use of leverage. Many experts point to excessive margin leverage on Wall Street, sometimes up to 95 percent, as a key to the collapse of 1929.

As Dave Ramsey points out in *The Total Money Makeover*, if you want to be involved in debt, then be the lender, not the borrower.[9] Governments or big corporations ask millions of people to give them little "loans," called bonds, and they pay interest on those loans to the bondholder. Perhaps you can't make loans like a bank, but you can purchase bonds. Bonds are loans.

The truth be known, in most instances, debt is bad, but some debts are tolerable. Here are three instances where this is the case:

- A mortgage on a house, especially if the note is a maximum of seven years
- A car loan for two years or less
- A student loan, where your expected future compensation is clearly able to repay the debt quickly

Let's take a look at these three situations in detail.

1. A Seven-Year-Maximum Mortgage

Where did we come up with the idea for the maximum loan you should incur being seven years of less? Actually, it's not a new idea at all.

A Brief History of Home Mortgages in the United States. Mortgages are incredibly common in the United States. In fact, according to the U.S. Census Bureau, approximately 70 percent of homes in the United States are mortgaged, with the remaining 30 percent being owned free and clear.[10]

Quick definition: A mortgage is a loan collateralized by real property (a single-family house, for the purposes of this chapter) through the use of a mortgage contract, which outlines the loan and the conditions under which the house is pledged to the lender until the loan is repaid. In everyday usage, "mortgage" generally refers to a mortgage loan. A home buyer or builder can secure a loan from a bank or other financial entity, and the loan contract will specify the size (amount of money), maturity, interest rate, repayment method, and other terms.[11]

The average length of a mortgage today is approximately 30 years.[12] However, mortgages issued in the United States before the

1930s were very different. These pre-1930 loans almost all had variable (floating) interest rates, required very high down payments (50 percent), and had one-year maturities, meaning the homeowner was required to renegotiate the home mortgage each and every year. Some mortgages, depending on the borrower's credit and down payment, were available with terms from 5 to 10 years.

In 1933 the Home Owners' Loan Corporation (HOLC) was created by the Home Owners' Refinancing Act and signed into law by Franklin D. Roosevelt. With the creation of the HOLC, terms for mortgages changed drastically. Where loans previously were variable-rate, short-term, nonamortizing mortgages, home buyers (or mortgage refinancers) could now find government-issued, fixed-rate, long-term (20-year) fully amortizing mortgages. (An "amortizing" mortgage is one where the principal is repaid over the life of the loan, so the borrower does not face a large lump-sum payment at the end of the loan.) By 1936, the HOLC converted one million mortgages to the new fixed-rate, long-term, amortizing standard.[13]

At this point in U.S. history, the federal government did not wish to be the holder of home mortgages. But investors needed an incentive to invest in mortgages that might not pay back the full balance if the homeowner defaulted (a serious concern during the Depression). So the National Housing Act of 1934 created the Federal Housing Administration (FHA), which provides government-guaranteed mortgage insurance. Thus, if a borrower who has an FHA-insured mortgage were to default, the FHA would pay the owner of the mortgage up to 97 percent of the house's appraised value. The HOLC's and FHA's issuance of fixed-rate, amortizing, long-term mortgages helped eliminate the tyranny of short-term mortgages with lump-sum ("balloon") payments for the entire principal due at maturity. The HOLC and FHA were not created specifically to promote homeownership but to prevent a "frozen" mortgage market from forcing Americans to leave their existing homes. [14]

The creation of the FHA may have allowed millions of new home buyers to secure a mortgage, as the lender could rely on FHA insurance if the borrower defaulted. However, just because a 30-year or longer mortgage is available does not mean that it's the best choice!

What Can You Afford to Pay for a Mortgage? Many Americans, when they decide to purchase a house, spend just a few minutes determining how much they can afford on a monthly basis. In other words, they sit down at their kitchen table, add up their monthly paychecks and other income, subtract what they require for food, clothing, cable TV, and Internet, etc., and the remainder is their monthly available mortgage payment.

Leaving this typical "financial planning lite" process aside for a moment, let's assume that the available monthly mortgage payment is $2,000. When our theoretical husband and wife meet their friendly neighborhood real estate agent, the agent's first question will be "How much were you thinking about spending on your new house?" Quickly the agent will calculate the amount the couple can pay, based on the monthly mortgage payment. For the most part, every mortgage is calculated based on this traditional formula (note that mortgages use compounding interest instead of simple interest):

$$M = P[i(1 + i)^n] / [(1 + i)^n - 1]$$

M = mortgage payment (monthly)
P = principal of the loan (original loan amount)
i = interest rate (r) divided by 12, or simply $r/12$
n = number of months until payoff (30-year mortgage = 12 months $\times$ 30 years = 360)

So, assuming a monthly mortgage payment of $2,000, an interest rate of 5 percent per year, and a 30-year term, the couple can purchase a $372,563 house.

Your House Really Costs Nearly Twice as Much. But wait. Generally a lender will require a down payment. Let's assume the couple has $50,000 in savings (or gifts from relatives) available to use toward the down payment. So now the requirement for financing is for the home purchase price less the down payment. Again, the real estate agent will incorporate this amount in the "value" of the home that the couple can purchase, and simply add the down payment onto the total amount that can be borrowed from the bank (as previously calculated). Thus, using the same assumptions, the couple can purchase a home that costs $422,563. At almost $425,000, this couple should be able to purchase a home in one of the top neighborhoods in most areas of the United States.

The next question is this: How much would the couple really be paying, over 30 years, for the privilege of borrowing the bank's money to finance the home purchase? You may be alarmed by the answer. If the monthly mortgage payment is $2,000 and the term of the loan is 30 years (360 months), then the couple would be paying $720,000 for the house! Not only that, since the couple put $50,000 down on the original purchase, they are really paying $720,000 + $50,000, or $770,000. Remember, the purchase price of the house was originally $422,563, so the interest on the mortgage would be the difference between the total paid and the purchase price, or $347,437. The interest, therefore, is over 82 percent of the original cost of the house.

Further, since the couple will be paying their mortgage each month for 30 years, they may not have the ability to save for retirement or other needs.

A Seven-Year Loan Saves a Million or More. Let's contrast the standard 30-year mortgage with our suggestion that you not take on debt, even a mortgage, of longer than seven years. We'll use the same assumptions of a monthly mortgage payment of $2,000 and an interest rate of 5 percent per year. With a seven-year term, the couple can purchase a $141,504 house. Adding the same $50,000 down payment, the total house purchase would be $191,504. When compared with the $422,563 house, that's a big difference!

Let's review how housing-related expenses over 30 years also might be different. Table 6.1 compares the expenses that change with the value of the house, such as property taxes. It ignores items such as cable TV, Internet access, and phone costs, since the couple will require those services regardless of the size or cost of the house.[15]

Although the higher-priced home allows the couple a larger income tax deduction for the property taxes and mortgage interest deduction, the total costs for the $422,563 house exceed $10,500 annually, while the costs for the $191,504 house are under $5,000 annually. That's a difference of almost $500 per month, just in extra costs.

Now let's address the elephant in the room: Do you really want to purchase a $191,504 house if you can "afford" a house that costs

TABLE 6.1 7-Year Mortgage vs. 30-Year Mortgage: Annual and Monthly Expenses

—	30-YEAR	7-YEAR	ASSUMED RATE*
Property taxes	$5,282.04	$2,393.80	1.25%
Repairs, maintenance	$4,225.63	$1,915.04	1.00%
Tax deductions	($12,676.90)	($5,745.11)	−3.00%
Furnishings	$5,282.04	$2,393.80	1.25%
Heat, A/C	$2,112.82	$957.52	0.50%
Insurance	$6,338.45	$2,872.59	1.50%
Total	**$10,564.08**	**$4,787.64**	**2.50%**
Difference		($5,776.44)	
Monthly difference		($481.37)	

*The assumed rate is the annual cost for each item expressed as a percentage of the cost of the house. For example, the 30-year mortgage for $422,563 will have property taxes of $5,282.04 (or 1.25% × $422,563).

$422,563? Probably not. The higher-priced home will likely be much bigger, in a "better" neighborhood, with access to better schools and other amenities. For example, it may be closer to your employer and thus offer a shorter commute. However, think about this: By purchasing the lower-priced home today, the couple in this example would be saving almost $500 per month in costs and paying off their mortgage 23 years earlier! They can then take the $2,000 per month they would have been using for their mortgage and save it. If we assume their investments earn 8 percent per year for 23 years, they'll have $1,577,462. Yes, you read that correctly—almost *$1.6 million* saved for retirement at the exact same time they would otherwise be sending in their final mortgage payment.

Is it possible to use a 15-year mortgage and get halfway to both goals? Sure. The longer the mortgage with a fixed monthly payment, the more you can spend on a house. Of course, the longer the mortgage, the longer you'll be paying for the mortgage. During that time, instead of saving money for your own retirement, you'll be paying the bank considerable interest and higher monthly costs for upkeep of your higher-priced home.

2. A Two-Year-Maximum Car Loan

This situation with car loans is the same story as a mortgage except you are dealing with a car salesman or saleswoman instead of a real estate agent. The salesperson will ask, "How much can you pay per month?" and then run your response through a formula, coming up with a figure as to how long you can incur debt for your car. Five years is not an uncommon response.

Two years, however, should be the maximum you extend yourself for an automobile. If you cannot finance your vehicle in two years, consider a different car. (Note that a late-model used car in excellent condition is often 40 percent cheaper than the same new car.)

A car loan is a secured loan, meaning the car itself is the asset that secures the loan. But car loans are far riskier than home loans because cars decrease in value over time while houses' values usually increase. Suppose you can't make your car payments any longer: Can you simply hand your car over to the bank and call it even?

No. It looks more like this: You hand over your car for which you owe $10,000. The bank is able to sell it for $3,000. You still owe the bank $7,000, and the bank will continue to hound you for the money. When you finally reach a place in life where you can afford a nice car again, that bank from your past will still be there, demanding the $7,000 you still owe, plus interest!

While car loans can be tolerable if necessary for transportation to work, they are intolerable unless the car is reasonably priced relative to your ability to pay it off completely in two years or less.

3. Student Loans

Debt that is secured by something you can see generating the revenues needed to pay the debt in a finite period of time is a good use of debt. Mortgages and education loans both fall under this category.

Many successful people had to borrow money to go to college. They knew they were going to get a better job because of their college or graduate school degrees and therefore planned ahead, incurring debt wisely. There are many studies that show the average college graduate earns at least six dollars more per hour than the non–college graduate. The extra amount made over a lifetime wildly exceeds the amount borrowed for college.[16]

How much will you or should you borrow for college? Most people would tell you that attending an elite school or an Ivy League college is worth every penny. Is it? In 2006, over half of the CEOs of the 50 biggest U.S. companies graduated from public colleges. Only four had graduated from Ivy League schools. The path to success does not have to be through Harvard.[17]

Going to an elite school makes no sense if it will bankrupt you later in life. (It may be worse than bankruptcy, as student loans cannot easily be erased if you declare bankruptcy.[18]) As of 2011,

Harvard costs in excess of $50,000 a year.[19] When all is said and done, certain schools might cost over $200,000! Warren Buffett graduated from the University of Nebraska–Lincoln.[20] The cost of attending this school is $7,400 per year. The difference in cost is obviously staggering.[21]

So consider a state college or university. A lot of students in college want to have a good time, right? Not surprisingly, they go out late at night and stay up to all hours of the morning, occasionally showing up late to, or entirely missing, an 8:00 A.M. class. And what would the cost of that single class session be at Harvard? About $300! That's the entire cost of a course at some state universities.

Credit Cards? No Way

The amount of credit card debt people willingly take onto their shoulders is astounding. Unlike the other three examples we looked at, credit card debt is not good debt in any way, especially if it is a result of poor spending, cash advances, and irresponsible business decisions. Many people use their credit cards as an attempt to live outside of their means, later finding that once they fall into such debt, it is nearly impossible to get out. Consider the following examples from a message board where credit counselors swap their clients' financial horror stories:

"How much credit card debt do you have?" asked Mark, a credit counselor, to his Asian client, who had started a film-processing company with her husband. The couple's business had gone belly-up with the advent of digital cameras. He thought the woman responded, "About fifteen." But her thick accent concealed the real number of thousands: "One hundred fifty." It turns out the Japanese couple had such high standards of honor regarding repaying their lease, they took out advances on their credit cards in the final two years of their business.

Another counselor posted that his current "record" was a client with over $175,000 in credit card debt, with the expected astronomical interest rates. His client had 25 credit cards. "I've got you beat," responded another counselor, who worked with a client owing $272,000 in unsecured debt. But a counselor from Austin, Texas, topped them: "My record is $317,000 in credit card debt for a debtor who made about $55,000 a year."

A counselor named Stephen, however, truly boasted the top figure. He worked with a dentist owing $496,000—nearly half a million dollars of personal credit card debt. But that was not the most astounding account, which instead belonged to Joseph, a Chapter 7 trustee, who was counseling a woman owing $125,000 on credit cards. Her income was $8,000 a year from Social Security.[22]

A Culture of Debt

At this point, you may be thinking, "OK, I'm convinced that debt is generally not desirable for me personally." However, debt permeates the U.S. culture, from corporations to states and municipalities, to the U.S. federal government, so a brief discussion of bigger "societal debt" issues would be helpful for context and to understand how our society has become so reliant on debt.

Exorbitant debt is alive and well in the corporate world. U.S. companies, according to *Business Week*, hold three times as much debt today as they did in 2001. The *USA Today* newspaper company recently reported $3.5 billion in debt the previous year with only $1.1 million in cash flow. During that same time, several well-known giants defaulted on their debt and declared bankruptcy, among them General Motors and Eddie Bauer.[23]

The average American does not seem to have the gumption at this point in history to stop utilizing debt, and neither does the American government. As of March 2010, the figure for the U.S. debt was $12.44 trillion.[24] The interest payment was $253 billion in 2008, nearly one-fifth of the entire budget. The debt is expected to nearly double again by 2010. We will spend more money in debt interest than we do on the military.[25] If the trend is not stopped, there are only two options:

1. Default. This means the United States goes bankrupt and tells its debtors it just can't or won't pay them back what they promised. David Walker, U.S. comptroller general from 1998 to 2008, provides insights regarding the size of the national debt:

> The national debt, as we speak, is about $10.5 trillion. But the real problem is not that number. The number that we need to be focusing on is the total federal financial hole; that's the total liabilities and unfunded promises for Social Security and Medicare. As of the end of 2007, which is the latest set of financials that we have right now, it was $53 trillion. That's $455,000 per household. Median household income in America is less than $50,000 a year.
>
> For the first time in the history of the United States, the federal financial hole exceeded the total net worth of all Americans. . . . So we could confiscate every dime of the net worth of every American household—including Warren Buffett, Bill Gates, and every other billionaire—and we wouldn't fill the hole. And guess what? The hole is getting deeper more rapidly than our net worth is going up.[26]

Walker's sobering account shows that bankruptcy—or simply being unable to pay our creditors—may be on the horizon.

Many of us have an elderly relative who doesn't trust the stock market, or growth mutual funds, or various business ventures worth investing in. He or she, let's call her Hattie, invests instead in U.S. Treasury bills. The return is low, maybe 1 or 2 percent, but Hattie feels safe beyond measure that her money will not disappear as it did for all those greedy fools who lost half their savings in the stock market in 2008.

Hattie is where the federal government currently gets the money it needs to operate beyond its means. So the federal government wants two wars and an overhauled health care system but has no money for it in the budget? They simply ask Hattie to send in her money, and they "promise" to give it back with interest sometime down the road.

Since there are millions of Hatties, that's a good chunk of change. But there are not nearly enough Hatties. So giant pension funds and major corporations also send their money to the U.S. government for T-bills, bonds, etc., just as Hattie does. But that is still not enough, so foreign governments also buy our Treasury certificates, just in case their currencies take a dive. As a Mexican, would you prefer to trust the U.S. government to pay you back, or would you instead believe your Mexican pesos will keep their value?

The largest owner of U.S. debt (Treasuries) is the nation of China. Foreign governments now purchase 75 percent of all new U.S. Treasuries that are sold to keep cash in the U.S. coffers.[27] Like Hattie, these governments expect to be able to get their money back from the United States with a small amount of interest.

So if the United States reached the point where it defaulted on all its debts, here's what would happen:

◆ Hattie would be very upset. The younger Hatties might riot.
◆ Pension funds across the country would collapse.
◆ Countries would respond with penalties, varying from economic tariffs to war.

A default by the federal government on its debt would be financially catastrophic and politically devastating, so it is unlikely. That's why the real threat is option two.

2. Massive Inflation. When the interest payments on the national debt prohibit us from paying bills like welfare, Social Security, Medicare, and defense (which would lead to rioting in the streets), then the government will resort to an age-old practice: printing more money.

In the age of digital money, the inflation of the currency won't be primarily by printing greenbacks but by changing the digits on the computer screen. It doesn't matter. Either way, when we thought we had only $500 to pay for the mortgage, car, and groceries, by golly it looks like we have $2,000! Everybody else also has $2,000 instead of $500. However, the grocery store still has only 50 jars of peanut butter on its shelves, and if the manager there doesn't double the price from $1 to $2, they will all disappear in one day, and lots of people will be mad. And if the store doesn't double the price, it won't be able to buy meat, because the cattle ranchers have doubled their prices for the same reason. So a dollar isn't what it used to be. It's half of what it used to be. It can only buy half a jar of peanut butter, not one jar.

On the plus side, this is handy for dealing with the national debt. The deals made with the Chinese were inked in a while back. We can pay their debt back with all these new dollars that have appeared, and they can't raise the price. But what they can do, along with Hattie and everyone else who has bought U.S. Treasuries in the past, is stop purchasing the Treasuries.

This will be the day of reckoning, when Americans are forced to spend only the cash they have on hand. To get more cash, the U.S. government must raise taxes or make very unpopular cuts to the biggest items in the budget. Meanwhile, the economy will be declining because a dollar isn't what it used to be.

The only way to get those folks like Hattie and the Chinese government to buy U.S. Treasuries again is to raise the interest rate of return: say, from 1 percent to 20 percent. So Hattie and the Chinese will get a lot more money back from their investment. But that also means when you buy a house or a car, your interest rate will be even higher than 20 percent.

Senior government officials agree with this possible scenario. "Here's the fundamental problem: How much money can a society borrow before it begins to have negative effects on our ability to borrow any more?" asks Paul O'Neill, who resigned as George W. Bush's secretary of the treasury in 2002 over the issue of a looming national debt. "When you get to the point that people won't loan you any more money as a government, you've got a horrendous problem. And it's happened to governments—in Argentina, most famously, in recent times. Mexico was kind of in that situation until we gave them a very big loan."

O'Neill offered this prediction: "Now, what happens before that is governments raise the interest rates so that people will loan them money. . . . Unfortunately, when interest rates get that high, economic activity slows down, and eventually it will stop. . . . China, India, Western Europe, even Central Europe—are going to have better places to invest their money than the United States because the currencies will be more sound than ours and the inflation rates will be lower."[28]

Option two, massive inflation, is a viable option for America. High inflation and interest rates already happened in the United States in the 1970s. Inflation also ruined Germany after World War I, when a loaf of bread cost a wheelbarrow full of Germany's paper currency.

The better idea is to never go into debt, personally, corporately, or nationally. Debt is always bad.

Secured Debt Is the Best Policy for Uncle Sam

Governments should try to follow the same principles as individuals: avoid unsecured debt whenever possible.

A good example of a secured government debt is a toll road. An example would be the Dallas North Tollway (DNT). This road provides safe, convenient passage in and out of downtown Dallas.[29] The tolls on the DNT pay for the maintenance of the road and pay off bonds used to create additional roads. This is a very good use of debt; it is securitized by the asset itself, the highway, which has value to the people who drive back and forth and are willing to pay for the privilege.

Another example is an airport. Sometimes such efforts can seem suspect, such as the $5 billion airport built 45 minutes outside of Denver, which ended up having baggage-handling issues and other problems. But even with all the problems, it is arguable that the airport increased Denver's productivity. The best way for government to justify borrowing money is to create something that will help generate future tax revenues and future general revenues for the larger economy.

Realistically, however, there will always be portions of government borrowing where no prospect for repayment is in sight. Programs such as Medicare, Medicaid, Social Security, and welfare are obvious examples. The military is another. Many Americans are not big advocates of the current wars we are fighting. That portion of the federal budget could be a lot smaller. Nevertheless, there is a need for a standing army, and the financing of the armed forces is another budget item that sometimes cannot be maintained without borrowed money.

As much as possible, a government's budget needs to go toward items that can be repaid in a reasonable amount of time. A reasonable amount of time is seven years or less.

Governments get into trouble when they borrow at excessive interest, knowing that this year's $100 item will cost $105 next year, and the government convinces itself it can simply raise taxes to cover the spread. What if the citizens in a struggling economy do not want to raise taxes? They rarely do in a thriving economy. At that point, at least with national governments, the choice is usually made to print or borrow more money.

Massive Inflation Is at Least a Decade Away

As pointed out earlier, too much is at stake for the United States to default on its massive debt. Slowly but surely, the federal government will continue to borrow more and continue to print more money, making inflation a larger problem. The dollar will lose significant value.

However, it is not likely that this will happen anytime soon. Be prepared for serious inflation by 2020 or 2025, but not anytime sooner. Why? Because the United States is still the safe haven for investors. Yes, America has its challenges, but most of the countries around the world still invest in the dollar and will continue to do so. Would you trust China with your money? How about Vladimir Putin in Russia? Europe, now the largest economy in the world, has to ask the same question. And the answer, for a decade or more, will continue to be no. They will trust the American dollar.

News reports talk about Russia and China and other nations developing a "basket of currencies" to replace the dollar as the world's reserve currency. That could happen, but it will take many years.

Another reason inflation will not hit us immediately is capacity underutilization. In other words, Americans will choose to be more productive rather than allow prices to go sky-high. Take the example of the $1 peanut butter jars on the shelf that might cost $2 in an economy with twice as much money. If one of the factory owners has a couple of peanut butter machines sitting idle, he may choose, instead of doubling prices, to make more jars of peanut butter. He may get people to work a third shift and make even more peanut butter. He can keep selling his jars for $1 or maybe $1.25, and the volume allows him to continue making a profit. His competitor, who expected to enjoy a cartel's profit, realizes, "Hey, I guess I can't raise prices."

Nevertheless, a day of reckoning will eventually come to all who borrow excessively. That includes the United States government, and that includes you and me.

The question should not be "How much debt should I have?" The better question is, "How much money should I save?"

THE STRATEGY: RATHER THAN ACCRUING DEBT, ACCUMULATE SAVINGS

Leverage or debt may sound good. But borrowing for any purpose other than investment or education is putting yourself in a financial sinkhole! Instead, save and watch your retirement plan bloom.

In a previous strategy, we discussed how much you need to save in order to retire, above and beyond your Social Security income (which, if you are the kind of person who reads a book like this, is likely to provide much less than half of what you need). The basic formula used was the figure of 20 to 1. In other words, take the amount you need each year to live adequately, and then multiply that number by 20. That is the amount of money you need to retire.

For example, if you need $50,000 a year to live right now, you need to save 20 times $50,000, or $1 million, to retire. If you live on $20,000 a year, you need to save $400,000 to retire. If you spend $250,000 a year, you need $5 million.

Clearly, you need to save a lot of money in proportion to your income, regardless of your level. And in planning your quest to save enough money to reach this number, you need to think about several issues.

How Much Should I Save?

Statisticians and academics use various formulas to determine how much of your income you should save each year to reach your goal. Without getting technical, and to make it simple for this book, a good place to start is 10 percent. Save 10 percent of your income toward your goal.

Will My 401(k) Be Enough?

Because of several issues involving the "human factor," modern retirement funds in IRAs and 401(k)s are underperforming relative to traditional pension funds, which are available to 50 percent fewer Americans since 1988.[30] As discussed in Strategy #1, in traditional pension plans (also called defined-benefit plans), the employer made almost all the decisions. The employer enrolled the workers, made the contributions, and managed the assets before and after the employee retired. The only decision left to the employee was the age at which to retire.

In contrast, 401(k) plans provide great flexibility for workers. Today, the employee decides whether or not to enroll, whether or not to contribute, how to invest the assets while employed at the company, and how to invest the assets while retired. Because of all these choices, 401(k) plans have proven to be far less effective than defined-benefit plans in steering Americans toward effective accumulation upon retirement. One-fifth of those eligible for 401(k) plans do not even enroll. According to some surveys, only 37 percent of those enrolled contribute to their pension. Approximately 10 percent contribute the maximum amount allowable.[31]

Pension assets are greatly decreasing. In theory, a pensioner who makes approximately $50,000 per year and contributes 6 percent regularly to his or her 401(k) over 30 years, and is matched with 3 percent by the company, should accumulate $320,000 for retirement. However, the Federal Reserve's Survey of Consumer Finances calculates that the typical individual accumulated only $78,000 upon retirement. This frightful decline in pension saving is compounded by the even scarier rate of savings accomplished by Americans outside of pension plans. In fact, in recent years, saving outside of pensions has been negative. Accumulating debt has outpaced accumulating assets.[32]

Get Those Matching Funds

If you work for a company that has a 401(k) plan and it matches the first 3 percent, for example, of your contributions, tax-deferred, then you simply must take advantage of such a great opportunity. Many readers will say, "I just don't have the extra money. I can't afford to do that." The response to such a statement is this: *you can't afford not to.*

Suppose you make $75,000 a year. If you saved 3 percent ($2,250) and your company contributed the match of an additional 3 percent, or $2,250, your annual contribution to your 401(k) would be $4,500. If you deferred that amount for 20 years and assumed an 8.5 percent growth rate, you would reach

$218,000. Note that by yourself, you would have contributed only $45,000.

Keep Your Tax-Deferred Accounts Until Retirement Age

As your 401(k) or IRA builds over time, always resist the temptation to cash it in. (As noted in Strategy #5, you should create your own personal emergency fund for times of desperation, so that cash is available somewhere to prevent you from dipping into your tax-deferred retirement accounts.) Cashing in a 401(k) or IRA remains one of the largest problems for increasing the numbers of at-risk Americans. Studies show that fully 45 percent of employees are cashing out their funds when they change jobs, and job changes are now occurring every four years.

Participants in retirement plans cashed out their assets even though they took a 10 percent tax penalty. According to the Center for Retirement Research, "Cashing out even small amounts can have a detrimental effect on ultimate accumulations. . . . The only way to end up at retirement with significant accumulations is to put the money into the account and leave it there. The prevalence of cashing out suggests that people do not get serious about saving for retirement until later in life, at which point it is very difficult to accumulate adequate amounts."[33]

But even if no emergency fund is available and you think you have to break into your 401(k) or IRA, think instead about borrowing against it. For example, if you have $50,000 in a 401(k), not only must you pay standard taxes on that money (say, 30 percent), you also pay a 10 percent penalty for early withdrawal. Your $50,000 immediately becomes $30,000. However, if you borrow against the money in your 401(k) at an interest rate of 10 percent against the entire $50,000, that would only cost you $10,000 in interest if you found a way to pay yourself back in two years. That's less than half as expensive. **Please note, this is not recommended, but it does show just how bad of an idea it is to take an early withdrawal from your retirement funds.**

Invest Your Retirement Accounts Wisely

Make sure the money in your 401(k) or IRA is invested properly. Modern regulations provide a good bit of flexibility on how to invest your money inside retirement accounts. You can use stocks, bonds, money market accounts, etc. You may also have opportunity to buy company stock. As discussed in Strategy #4, hiring a professional financial adviser, who is charged with the fiduciary responsibility of putting your own interests first, is the best decision when seeking investment advice.

Postpone the Age of Retirement

Think about retiring later, which would allow you to work longer and save more before you begin the process of pulling money out of your portfolio. Every additional year you work really does affect the numbers significantly. Now, I am not saying you should wait until you've spent all your golden years working and then retire 20 minutes before you die. But think of your career as having different stages.

Do you have more to contribute to your industry or related industries? If you love your current field, maybe you can work a few more years full-time or even several more years part-time. Consider the company YourEncore, which helps certain professionals achieve semiretired status. As a member of the company, a retiree's expertise is sold to firms such as Eli Lilly, Procter & Gamble, and General Mills for 10 to 20 hours per month.[34] By working as a consultant after you have retired, you may be able to experience retired life while still earning income.

If you don't particularly like your job and are counting the days until you can quit, perhaps there are other productive tasks and realms of activity you do enjoy. You could get involved as a volunteer or a part-time worker 10 years or so before retirement, and when the day job is behind you, perhaps you can find a way to earn some income related to the kind of work you really do enjoy.

Can't Cut Costs? Earn More Money

Many families and individuals say, "I make $25,000 a year," or $75,000 a year, or $150,000 a year—whatever it is, "and I need every single penny. I cannot possibly save."

This book was not written to debate that. It may be the case. It can be very difficult to go down a family budget and say, "We need to cut this by 10 percent to save money." It's hard to say, "I can't go to Starbucks ever, ever, ever. Maybe I can go two days instead of four days a week." (Disclaimer: The author has a daily Starbucks habit.) Cutting expenses can often result in battles between spouses or conflicts with children.

Instead of always looking at the expense side of the equation, perhaps it is much easier to think about increasing your revenue. There are many ways to do it:

◇ Work overtime at your job.
◇ If you work for yourself, find more opportunities in your area.
◇ If you stay at home, is there something you can do for an hour a day to earn extra money?
◇ Is there something you can do while watching TV?
◇ Is a part-time job available?

This is not to say that you must go out and work at a fast-food restaurant or a convenience store during the midnight shift. Just look around you. Opportunities are everywhere.

Social Security Is Not Nearly Enough: You Must Save

Look for ways to make more money. Look for ways to cut costs. Save, save, save. Every bit saved now gains interest and compounds to help you in the future. Take advantage of company-matched contributions. Allow a financial professional to help you wisely invest in your 401(k) or IRA, so your investments can grow successfully. And always avoid the temptation to withdraw early and get killed by taxes and penalties. You should spend the last decade of your career making sure your debts will be paid off before you begin taking money out of your savings.

Saving is great. And aside from a few tolerable exceptions, debt is always bad.

STRATEGY #6 Checklist

☑ Be debt free when you retire.

☑ Cut current expenses, postpone retirement, or work a second job to be debt free by retirement.

☑ Contribute to your 401(k), and verify that your employer contributes matching funds, if available.

☑ Give your licensed financial professional copies of your 401(k) and company IRA statements, so he or she can advise you on which products to invest in.

Utilize Annuities and Other Strategies to Account for Longevity and Health Care

THE MISCONCEPTION: HEALTH AND LONG-TERM CARE WILL BE AVAILABLE AND FREE FOR ALL

The new health care reform act, the Health Care and Education Reconciliation Act of 2010 (Pub. L. 111-152, 124 Stat. 1029), offers "universal coverage" and "comprehensive health care reform." The act is considered "the biggest expansion of the U.S. federal government's social safety net since the 1960's." According to MSNBC:

> The bill . . . will bring near-universal coverage to a wealthy country in which tens of millions of people are uninsured. It makes Obama the first president to succeed in passing comprehensive health care reform since Teddy Roosevelt championed the cause a century ago.

The measure represents the biggest expansion of the U.S. federal government's social safety net since the 1960s, when President Lyndon B. Johnson enacted the Medicare and Medicaid government-funded health care coverage programs for the elderly and poor.[1]

There's even better news if you live in Massachusetts!

This year, more than 98 percent of Massachusetts residents have health insurance. These results are astonishing. Some of the most exciting news is related to children and elderly adults, as the survey found that virtually all Massachusetts children have health insurance (99.8 percent) and nearly all elderly adults are covered (99.6 percent). The survey, conducted by the independent Urban Institute on behalf of the Division [Massachusetts Division of Health Care Finance and Policy], indicates that coverage is very strong for Massachusetts residents at all income levels, ranging from 96 percent for those with family income under 300 percent of the federal poverty level to over 99 percent of those with income above 500 percent of the federal poverty level.[2]

In fact, we won't have any increasing costs to contend with in the future, as "cutting costs" actually results in better care! The *New York Times* reports on health care cost reductions in Richmond, Virginia:

Since 1996, the Richmond area has lost more than 600 of its hospital beds, mostly because of state regulations on capacity. Several hospitals have closed, and others have shrunk. In 1996, the region had 4.8 hospital beds for every 1,000 residents. Today, it has about three. Hospital care has been, in a word, rationed.[3]

The article goes on to discuss how the quality of care in Richmond continues to improve and is already better than in most

U.S. metropolitan areas. Medicare data for the city shows that Richmond hospitals perform a "better-than-average job" of treating pneumonia, heart attacks, and heart failure. When patients in Richmond were queried as to whether they felt their health care had been rationed, respondents were positive. Retired school district employee Janet Binns said, "I feel like there's nothing cheap about the care." Binns provided the example that when her elderly father fell down one morning, all she had to do was e-mail a doctor who responded within minutes and was on the phone with her moments later.

So stop worrying about saving for expected higher health care costs in your retirement future. Not only will the government continuously improve care, it will also pay for everything!

THE TRUTH: WITH INCREASED LONGEVITY, HEALTH CARE COSTS WILL BE A SUBSTANTIAL PORTION OF YOUR BUDGET

Health care reform, Obamacare, universal coverage—there is so much media attention to our nation's health care debate that even the so-called experts get confused. While so many improvements can be made to our current system, universal coverage without cost to the patient or taxpayer is unlikely now or in the future.

Massachusetts took the first step toward universal care when its health insurance reform law was enacted in 2006. This law requires that almost every resident obtain some minimum amount of health insurance coverage, or face a fine. There are considerable state-funded subsidies for residents earning up to three times the federal poverty level. While some differences exist between the recent federal legislation and the Massachusetts version, the state's experience might be viewed as indicative of the future for health insurance in the United States as a whole.

It's difficult to pick up a magazine or newspaper or even open your Internet browser without being deluged with opinions on the health care law, legal challenges, or expectations for the future. **Remember, whether or not the health care law "succeeds" is less important than whether you and those you care for, or support financially, have the health insurance coverage you or they require.**

One of the most consistent comparisons discussed between Massachusetts' health insurance legislation and the federal version is the requirement for universal purchase of health insurance while ignoring any system-wide cost reduction. It stands to reason that unless health insurance premiums, in aggregate, exceed the cost of providing health care, the health care system, whether specific to Massachusetts or to the United States as a whole, faces deficits. Once deficits accumulate, either premiums (direct costs to patients or taxpayer-funded subsidies) will increase, or health care costs (for doctors, hospitals, medications, etc.) must be reduced. It's just simple math. In his review of John E. Wennberg's *Tracking Medicine: A Researcher's Quest to Understand Health Care*, Arnold Relman writes:

> In this respect the federal reforms resemble the legislation passed in Massachusetts some four years ago that mandated near-universal coverage but made essentially no provisions for containing the costs that would inevitably ensue. Massachusetts is now struggling with its costs and is being forced to curtail health services.[4]

Shawn Tully echoes Relman's thoughts in a recent *Fortune* magazine article:

> The battle in Massachusetts may foreshadow the results of the new federal law. It threatens to mirror precisely the cycle we're witnessing in the Bay State: spiraling costs that make coverage unaffordable for both patients and businesses, followed by price controls that drive private providers from the market. "This could repeat itself on the national level, and become the begin-

ning of government-run health care," says Lora Pellegrini, chief of the Massachusetts Association of Health Plans.[5]

Someone has to pay for increasing health insurance coverage when the costs exceed insurance premiums. Tully writes:

> Costs are rising relentlessly for both families and for the state government. The median annual premium for family plans jumped 10% from 2007 to 2009 to $14,300—again, that's a substantial rise on top of an already enormous number. For small businesses, the increase was 12%. In 2006, the state spent around $1 billion on Medicaid, subsidies for medium-to-lower earners, and other health-care programs. Today, the figure is $1.75 billion. The federal government absorbed half of the increase.[6]

What happens when Massachusetts finds itself facing escalating health care costs? The commonwealth's elected officials divert tax revenues to cover those higher costs, at the expense of other items. As in many other states, Massachusetts law requires an annual balanced budget.[7] If a balanced budget is required by law and health care costs are increasing, funding for schools, state and municipal employees, infrastructure, disaster readiness, and the like must be reduced, unless taxes rise to cover the shortfall.

Robert J. Samuelson expressed a similar view recently in the *Washington Post*, where he described Massachusetts' budget challenges related to health care coverage:

> Aside from squeezing take-home pay (employers provide almost 70 percent of insurance), higher costs have automatically shifted government priorities toward health care and away from everything else—schools, police, roads, prisons, lower taxes. In 1990, health spending represented about 16 percent of the state budget, says the Massachusetts Taxpayers Foundation. By 2000, health's share was 22 percent. In 2010, it's 35 percent. About 90 percent of the health spending is Medicaid.[8]

Can't Something Be Done?

If there is enough pressure on the health care system to contain costs and reduce spending, won't someone or some organization find a way to provide health care less expensively? Doesn't America have a history of innovation? Perhaps in the long run. However, the trend for health care costs isn't lower or even neutral; it's sharply higher in recent years. Further, the "system" appears to be moving away from cost containment and toward revenue maximization for the health care provider, causing expenses to rise still faster.

In the *New Yorker* magazine, Dr. Atul Gawande describes how the cost of providing health care in the United States is already the highest in the developed world. His articles on higher-cost regions, such as southern Texas, and the predictions for the future of health care costs are sobering: "The explosive trend in American medical costs seems to have occurred here [McAllen, Texas] in an especially intense form. Our country's health care is by far the most expensive in the world. . . . Spending on doctors, hospitals, drugs, and the like now consumes more than one of every six dollars we earn."[9]

According to Gawande, the financial issues the United States is facing are having major negative results on the global competitiveness of its businesses, while bankrupting millions of its families, even those who may have insurance. The cost of medical care and health insurance is also creating huge issues for our government. Gawande quotes President Barack Obama in a March 2009 speech: "The greatest threat to America's fiscal health is not Social Security. It's not the investments that we've made to rescue our economy during this crisis. By a wide margin, the biggest threat to our nation's balance sheet is the skyrocketing cost of health care. It's not even close."[10]

Dr. Gawande goes on to describe a major obstacle to efficient and affordable health insurance: the current health care system itself. Unfortunately, the recent federal health care legislation does little to address the system and its incentives:

Providing health care is like building a house. The task requires experts, expensive equipment and materials, and a huge amount of coordination. Imagine that, instead of paying a contractor to pull a team together and keep them on track, you paid an electrician for every outlet he recommends, a plumber for every faucet, and a carpenter for every cabinet. Would you be surprised if you got a house with a thousand outlets, faucets, and cabinets, at three times the cost you expected, and the whole thing fell apart a couple of years later? Getting the country's best electrician on the job (he trained at Harvard, somebody tells you) isn't going to solve this problem. Nor will changing the person who writes him the check.[11]

Increased Longevity

Exacerbating this health care issue is the fact that Americans are living longer than ever before. It is likely that you will live much longer than your parents. Life expectancy is increasing sharply, and you need to prepare yourself for several more years of senior living than the years for which you or your parents previously planned.

Recently the established and highly credible Society of Actuaries has processed the data and provided the prognosis in its *Risks and Process of Retirement Survey Report.* In the year 1900, when a man reached 65, he could expect to live another 11.4 years, according to the Society of Actuaries. But in 2050, he can expect to live 19 years longer. Retirement years are steadily increasing. Before, if you were lucky enough to live to 85, you could expect to live another 3.7 years. In 2050, it will be almost double at 6.3 years.

For females, the numbers are more drastic. In 2050, if a woman reaches age 65, she can expect to live another 21½ years. That's age 86. Statistically her grandmother would have made it only to age 77.[12] Will you, your spouse, or one of your parents live to age 90? Today, the numbers show nearly a 50 percent chance of one of your parents making it to age 90 if both are currently alive. In 2025, the chances increase to nearly 60 percent.[13] That's a huge jump in such a short time, whether those numbers apply to your parents, or, by that time, to you and your spouse.

Times Change

One hundred years ago, most Americans had a simple retirement plan: "I am going to have a lot of kids, and they will support me when I'm old. Either I'll live with them, or they will bring me food next door."

These Americans did not have a 30-year mortgage. Neither did they have credit card debt nor monthly cell phone bills. Their children made them as comfortable as possible as they grew older, got sick, and eventually died. There was not a worry regarding enormous health care expenses, because today's advanced medical equipment and procedures did not exist.

The cost of retirement was much lower. In fact, you could argue that you did not need to save anything if your children were there to take care of you. You just had to get through your adult life with your own children and take care of your own parents, who probably died when you were in your 50s, or maybe even your 40s.

If you worked for a corporation in those days, it gave you a pension and defined benefits. This was also true for all government workers: teachers, firefighters, emergency workers, police, postal workers, and the armed forces. Defined benefits are basically gone now. Though they still exist for those who worked in the past, now in their 70s or 80s, today's middle-aged workers generally either have no pension or manage their own retirement accounts in individual retirement accounts (IRAs) or 401(k) plans.

Senior living is looming in our future. If you fail to plan, you can plan on failing. This fact requires specific action in order to prepare for longevity. Have you ever heard the expression "If I had known I was going to live this long, I would have taken better care of myself"? Since you know you'll be around for a while, take a few minutes to start implementing the following powerful rules.

THE STRATEGY: UTILIZE ANNUITIES AND OTHER STRATEGIES TO ACCOUNT FOR LONGEVITY AND HEALTH CARE

Not only do you need a private pension today to replace the traditional pensions no longer available, you need that private pension to be solid and well funded.

You are going to live a long, long time. Even if you think you are in perfect health, you probably would benefit from long-term care insurance. The statistics regarding those in old age who experience chronic illness are likely to catch up with you. A report issued by the Society of Actuaries contained another piece of alarming information for our generation about premature retirement: "About 40% of Americans end up retiring earlier than they planned, usually as a result of job loss, family needs and health issues, or poor personal health. This further aggravates the already serious risks associated with longevity."[14]

In this book, we focus on some foundational girders to successfully reach retirement, including a goal of accumulating 20 years' worth of today's income in retirement funds. Another goal is six months of savings socked away in liquid assets as an emergency fund for difficult days that might eat away your savings. (Don't forget the 20–7–6 rule.)

These two strategies are difficult in themselves. But if nearly half of Americans are retiring years earlier than expected, the goal becomes much more complicated. This situation is a big deal, and it is a major crisis. What are these people going to do? How will they make it? Regarding retirement, this may be the big cultural question for our times.

Get Back to the Fundamentals

Americans love quick fixes. They like to check the box and watch their problems go away. Remember when Procter & Gamble created Olestra, the fat substitute? As a country, we had a problem with gaining weight, so an easy solution was offered that allowed us to eat potato chips and crackers with no more consequences. That was a great quick fix for America. Unfortunately, it didn't work. We learned later that it was the carbohydrates, more than the fat, that made us gain weight.

Many people reading this book, some with very good incomes, are counting on a quick fix later in life in regards to their retirement. They may think, "I'll retire in five years, and the market will go straight up." But the information in this section should scare you straight out of that unlikely strategy. Other people may adopt the ostrich mentality and just put their head in the sand. "I'm never going to save $5 million," they say, "so why bother saving anything at all? I guess I will just work for the rest of my life."

The best solution is to go back to the fundamentals, such as these:

- Find a way to save 20 years of your current annual income.
- Get out of debt.
- Secure your emergency fund.
- Work with your financial professional to help you reach your goals.

In addition, there is a particular financial vehicle that can be a strategic help to fight our generation's trends of longer life, more expensive medical care, and the likelihood of earlier-than-expected retirement: annuities. You should discuss annuities at length with your financial professional. He or she is likely to counsel you to invest in annuities to some degree.

Again, these are not silver-bullet solutions for your retirement challenges (there is *no* silver bullet), but they can be helpful to a degree. For that reason, the remainder of this strategy will discuss them a bit more.

An Annuity Can Serve as an Income Supplement

The word *annuity* seems to be fraught with emotion. The media have made annuities sound disadvantageous to the average consumer. Ask the average guy about an annuity. Eight out of ten are likely to say annuities are just a product that some insurance guy wants to sell you to rip you off. This thought couldn't be further from the truth. Annuities can have real value.

First, we need to define an annuity: it is an investment that pays a stated amount of money for a stated period of time. Social Security, for example, is an annuity. A pension has similar qualities to an annuity: if you die, it dies with you. You get no extra money if you die early. (Note that some pensions provide for a "survivor's benefit" if selected by the pensioner prior to retirement. Social Security also provides survivor's benefits in certain cases.)

An annuity sold by an insurance company can act as a pension substitute. If you contribute so much per month or per year to an annuity, at some point down the road, the annuity kicks in and pays you $1,000, $2,000, or perhaps $5,000 a month for several years. If the annuity begins at age 65 and lasts 10 years, you have a pension-like income until you are 75. For those who have difficulty saving—those who, for whatever reason, usually watch their savings get spent—an annuity can be a helpful option for securing income in your later days.

Talk to your financial professional. Develop your financial plan. Figure out the minimum income you will need the day you want to retire. (This, of course, assumes you have paid off your credit card debt and burned your mortgage.) Figure out what else you need each month to live, and buy an annuity for that amount. Take the remainder of your money, and invest it appropriately: mutual funds, exchange-traded funds, bonds, money market funds, and other securities that can be sold quickly in the event you require cash quickly.

Longevity Insurance

You should consider the longevity risk annuity, sometimes referred to as longevity insurance, in addition to the previously described annuity. In the previous example, the annuity provided steady income until age 75. But what if you live much longer, as the trends surely suggest? What if you live to age 95?

Longevity insurance provides certain income every year of your life until you die. For example, you could purchase a longevity annuity for $50,000 today with the promise that $40,000 a year will come your way for the rest of your life, starting at age 65, 75, or 80. Obviously, the costs will vary depending on which age you choose as the starting point.

How can the insurance company afford such a deal? The answer is simple: some people don't live to age 75 (or whatever age you picked). Of those who do, some people do not live many years beyond age 75. But others live to age 100. The insurance actuaries know the risks and are willing to sell you an annuity, if you are willing to take the opposite risk. Some people prefer to have access to their money all their lives. Others are willing to take the risk of never seeing their money if they die early, but enjoy the security of a guaranteed income the rest of their lives, no matter how long they live.

Long-Term Care Insurance

Another product that warrants your consideration is commonly referred to as long-term care insurance (LTC). This type of insurance generally covers home care, assisted living, and nursing home care. LTC covers services generally not covered by health insurance, Medicare, or Medicaid. Many individuals feel uncomfortable relying on their family to be taken care of later in life and find that long-term care insurance could help cover out-of-pocket medical expenses. Without LTC, the cost of nursing home care could quickly deplete the savings of an individual or family.

Don't count on Medicare and Medicaid to cover all the expenses related to health care in later life. In fact, expect the costs to add up quite extensively. According to a study by the Employee Benefit Research Institute, the savings needed to ensure just a 50 percent chance of covering all health costs for a man until he dies is $86,000; for a woman, $126,000. For a 90 percent chance of success, the institute recommends health care savings of $177,000 for men and $221,000 for women.[15]

Expect health care costs to continue to increase at a high rate. Bud Hebeler, a former Boeing executive who now studies retirement finances, suggests that people "prepare a detailed retirement budget derived from current budgets—but use much larger medical and dental costs, perhaps 1.5 times today's insurance and service quotes, if these costs continue to run at twice normal inflation."[16]

STRATEGY #7 Checklist

☑ Expect to live longer. Analyze investments and insurance to protect yourself and your family from "elderly" expenses, such as health care.

☑ Consider whether annuities can fill the significant income gap between Social Security and your required retirement income. The purchase of an annuity causes automatic savings.

☑ The possibility of needing home care or assisted living increases as a person grows older. The purchase of long-term care insurance can offset the costs of these services.

Plan Your Legacy Through Children and Charity

THE MISCONCEPTION: THE AMERICAN DREAM IS TO KICK BACK AND NEVER WORK AGAIN

At the end of each episode of "Lifestyles of the Rich and Famous"—the mid-1980s to mid-1990s reality TV show highlighting the extravagance of the wealthy—host Robin Leach signed off with his classic and unforgettable phrase "Champagne wishes and caviar dreams."

Who of us has not dreamed of having the luck of Jed Clampett, the famous "Beverly Hillbillies" sitcom character whose good fortune led to some "bubblin' crude"? That oil he discovered on the back side of his farm allowed Jed to do what we all would like to do if we could retire early: head to the warm weather, buy a mansion, kick back, and swim in the pool all day.

But what makes America so great is that this is a nation where you don't have to simply rely on luck like Jed Clampett's.

In the United States, the ability to make your fortune, retire early, and relax is within your grasp. It's largely up to you as an individual to make the right choices, take some risks, strategize, and work hard toward your goals.

Frontier Individualism

This American dream has been forged successfully over more than four centuries, beginning with the conquest of the great American frontier. Starting with Plymouth and Jamestown, then Daniel Boone and Davy Crockett (who tamed the land by killing a bear simply with his hands), leading up to the thousands of families who embarked on the Oregon Trail, Americans have proved that luck was not the main ingredient to owning thousands of acres and creating generations of wealth. Instead, the key was individual choice and the right to private property.

At the World's Fair in 1893, University of Wisconsin professor Frederick Jackson Turner coined the phrase "rugged individualism." He explained to a group of scholars that Americans are a rugged, self-made race, forged in adversity through the pioneering experience, reborn and purified into a breed unique on earth. His paper later became the well-known work *The Frontier in American History.*[1]

This rugged American cleared wild forests and built one-room cabins for his family to dwell in for years. He hunted for food and planted crops, then harvested them with his own sharp tools and sold them. He risked, he worked, and he was rewarded.

Many American heroes fit the rugged profile: Andrew Jackson was known as Old Hickory, hard and hardheaded, apt to fight a fellow settler as often as a wild animal. Abe Lincoln grew up in a log cabin. Theodore Roosevelt led his Rough Rider cavalry into battle and, later in life, ventured into the yet-to-be-explored Amazon jungle. All these men found their star, and they deserved to enjoy the fruits of their success.

The Founding Fathers Believed in Your Property Rights

The Founding Fathers were well aware of the dignity of private property. James Otis, an early advocate of colonial rights, said in 1761, "One of the most essential branches of English liberty is the freedom of one's house. A man's house is his castle."

John Adams said private property is "as sacred as the laws of God." Thomas Jefferson further made it clear in the Declaration of Independence that no American should ever be deprived of "life, liberty, and the pursuit of happiness." And if there were any doubt as to what was meant by this statement, Jefferson's early drafts used the phrase "the pursuit of property."[2]

The website Indy.com asked in a poll what people would do if they were independently wealthy. "I would work on my golf game and on my tan on the beach," said one typical respondent. And rightly so. If you have achieved the American dream, you have the right to enjoy it.

There is nothing new under the sun, and we find that in the Bible, King Solomon, known as the wisest man in the world, had the same idea of enjoying life. In Ecclesiastes 8:15 (NIV), Solomon says, "So I commend the enjoyment of life, because nothing is better for a man under the sun than to eat and drink and be glad."

Of course, it takes money to be able to eat and drink and be glad. That is what makes the American dream so wonderful: you do not have to be some aristocrat or a person of social standing. Any common person, through planning and hard work, has the opportunity of finding his or her fortune. It's all about the Golden Rule: he who has the gold rules.

Rush to Your Fortune

Rush Limbaugh is one of the great modern spokesmen for the American dream. (Let's ignore the politics for a moment.) He has modeled it himself, starting as a typical middle-class guy and escalating himself into a net worth of hundreds of millions.

"Rugged individualism is what built this country," says Limbaugh. "Rugged individuals have great and high expectations of themselves. It was rugged individualists that built the railroads. It was rugged individualists that discovered the New World. It was rugged individualists that dreamed about getting to the moon. It was rugged individualists that invented the automobile and the airplane, the bullet, the gun. It was rugged individualists who invented medicines, improvements in health care. It wasn't a bunch of groups."[3]

While Boone and Crockett and Jackson and Lincoln were early models of the American dream, Limbaugh provides even more examples of rugged individuals and their accomplishments: "They're all working to try to be the best they can be and come out on top. Thomas Edison, the light bulb. Benjamin Franklin, electricity. Alexander Graham Bell, the telephone . . . Henry Ford, automobile mass production, the assembly line."[4]

Limbaugh articulates what Americans used to learn in the classroom in decades past: that free-market capitalism, the force that drives the world for good and prosperity, is generated by the individual's self-interest. The great Adam Smith, in his 18th-century classic *The Wealth of Nations*, called this principle the "invisible hand" of providence.

In the 21st century, however, says Limbaugh, self-interest has been misrepresented:

> Rugged individualism is portrayed, unfortunately, as selfishness. But it is not selfishness. Rugged individualism is self-interest, and self-interest is good. . . . Let's say you're a father, a husband. What is your self-interest? Well, if you take it responsibly, the responsibility of being a husband and father, your self-interest is improving the life that your family lives. You want economic opportunity for them. You want social stability for them. . . .
>
> Without believing in yourself, you're going nowhere, and you won't believe in yourself if somebody beats the individual out of you. If somebody convinces you that you don't deserve to do better than anybody else because that's not fair, and they are teach-

ing you that in school about your grades and they're teaching you that about economics. It's not fair that you might have a nicer car than the schlub down the street. It's not fair. It's humiliating to the people who have less. So they're trying to beat the individual out of you, and the individual in you, the belief in yourself is the only thing you've got to compete against everybody that's trying to hold you back, and they all are. It's the way of the world.[5]

But the American hero resists this force. He or she competes, takes risks, makes good choices, and works incredibly hard. Today, many people continue to seize the American dream and are able to retire early. They can kick back, relax, and enjoy themselves for the remainder of their lives. They've earned it.

THE TRUTH: WE ARE ALL HERE TO WORK FOR A LIFETIME, NO MATTER WHAT WORK WE CHOOSE

The goal of this book is to help you reach financial independence. Once you get there, it is indeed your right to live however you wish, with no boss and especially no government authority telling you any differently. The higher road, however, and the better part of all wisdom, is to use your newfound time and freedom to remain as productive as possible, and to continue your legacy of working to make the world a better place.

Clearly, the sanctity of private property as defended by the Founding Fathers extends to all of those who have worked hard and taken risks to reach financial independence. Have you reached your number? Did your ship come in, as Jed Clampett's did? Then enjoy yourself. Throw some parties. Travel the world for a season. Eventually, however, that spirit deep within all humankind will be nagging at you to get on with more fulfilling tasks. Remember the age-old truth: personal fulfillment ultimately comes from giving, not receiving.

We already know this. The message of this truth is not a new idea. It is a reminder of what we learned when we moved from *being* children to *parenting* children. Somehow, the greater fulfillment is generated by becoming the parents who sacrifice for our children, not by being the children who enjoy a lot of fun. Without realizing it or not, at some point, we all crossed that threshold where receiving gifts was eclipsed by the joy of watching others open the presents we had given them.

Nevertheless, the glitz and glamour of the world can be enticing, so we need consistent reminders that a life of constant pleasure does not fulfill us in the long run.

Consider ex-basketball stars Larry Bird and Michael Jordan: They both love golf, and they are both worth millions. Why don't they play golf all the time? Because great achievers, like these great athletes, need a real challenge. And like clockwork, after a couple of years of golf, they each moved into management, ownership, broadcasting, and journalistic pursuits. They keep working.

Early Retirement and Mortality

Keeping a mind focused on being productive throughout your life can also have health and longevity benefits. The *British Medical Journal* cites a study of thousands of employees who retired at various ages. The results showed that early retirement resulted in early mortality. Men who retired before age 55 were twice as likely to die earlier than those who retired in their 60s.[6] (We've all heard stories of the man who worked every day of his life but died a few weeks after he retired.) The trick is to stay active, involved, and productive, even as you pass the point of financial independence.

In fairness to the American heroes mentioned in the description of this strategy's misconception, all of them continued to stay productive throughout their lives. Rush Limbaugh could have retired five times over, but for better or worse, he cannot keep himself out of the broadcasting booth.

It is fair to say that individuals with the kind of mentality that looks at the goal of financial independence as a means to stop producing may be much less apt to reach financial independence in the first place.

The Wisest Man in the World

It is true that King Solomon, "the wisest man in the world," encouraged his readers in the Old Testament book of Ecclesiastes to "eat, drink, and be merry." He did so himself, enjoying wine, women (at least a thousand of them!), and every pleasure imaginable. In Ecclesiastes 2, he writes:

> I tried cheering myself with wine, and embracing folly—my mind still guiding me with wisdom. I wanted to see what was worthwhile for men to do under heaven during the few days of their lives. I undertook great projects: I built houses for myself and planted vineyards. I made gardens and parks and planted all kinds of fruit trees in them. I made reservoirs to water groves of flourishing trees. I bought male and female slaves and had other slaves who were born in my house. I also owned more herds and flocks than anyone in Jerusalem before me. I amassed silver and gold for myself, and the treasure of kings and provinces. I acquired men and women singers, and a harem as well—the delights of the heart of man. I became greater by far than anyone in Jerusalem before me. . . .
>
> In all this my wisdom stayed with me. I denied myself nothing my eyes desired; I refused my heart no pleasure. My heart took delight in all my work, and this was the reward for all my labor. Yet when I surveyed all that my hands had done and what I had toiled to achieve, everything was meaningless, a chasing after the wind; nothing was gained under the sun.[7]

For the wisest man in the world, the conclusion was that a quest for self-actualization and personal fulfillment only leads to depression. True fulfillment is derived from focusing on others, not ourselves.

THE STRATEGY: PLAN YOUR LEGACY THROUGH CHILDREN AND CHARITY

Someone once told me that you need to prepare well in advance for the next stage of your life—or you are going to have a heck of a time dealing with the next stage of your life.[8] For example, consider the transition from being single, or married with no kids, to the stage of having kids. Everyone looks back and says, "Wow, you can't believe what a change that is!" How do you prepare for that? Work for a local diaper service? Wake yourself up every hour in the middle of the night? More seriously, you can spend time with family and friends who have kids. You can baby-sit. You can start learning to cook more meals at home instead of eating out at restaurants.

The same kind of preparation needs to be made for the transition from working full-time to having more freedom, being able to contribute your time and money to any situation on the planet you so choose. It's easier to prepare for this while you are in the previous stage of life—similar to how it seems easier to find a job while you are employed.

Is Volunteering a Good Idea?

Is it a good idea to devote yourself to volunteer work? Maybe. Giving back through volunteering or financial contributions isn't for everyone, but if you find something to do that's easy and fun, you may realize you are enjoying yourself.

If you are interested in volunteering, it is important that you find ways to make time to do so while you are still in the prime of your earning capacity. This experience will grease the skids and provide practice for when you have the opportunity to dedicate a greater amount of time and effort.

If you don't know where to start, head to the United Way's volunteer center (http://www.volunteer-center.org), located in nearly every community, for a great list of places that need help. You may have opportunities at your house of worship, with charities nearby, or with groups your family is already involved with. Some people like putting on an apron and serving the homeless at a soup kitchen. But that kind of hands-on action is not for everybody.

Those of us who spend our time in the business world might feel much more comfortable volunteering as a board member, or what may be called an "administrative volunteer." Boards are quite easy to get on and off, they usually meet only once a month, and most charities have a great need for help at this level. The director of a charitable group may be great at passing out blankets but less adept when dealing with accounting statements, fundraising strategies, and legal matters. A retired professional can handle such issues in her sleep. Once you've dipped your toe in the water by serving on a board, you may want to get involved in more hands-on activities. Either way, you are preparing for when you have 24 hours a day to give your time to something larger than yourself.

Financial Preparations for Your Next Stage of Life

How are you preparing yourself for the next stage from a financial perspective? Do you have enough life insurance to be able to leave something for your children and also leave a financial legacy to charity? Most people are wildly underinsured.

Suppose you have the capacity to be insured for $5 million. Wouldn't that be a much better thing to hand down to your children and others after you die than $500,000 in investments (the cost of the insurance)? That $500,000 in investments might get ravaged by inflation or any number of harmful trends. Life insurance, however, is incredibly efficient from a tax perspective and passes down the insurance money to the beneficiary tax free. It also passes to charities tax free and is exempt from the estate tax, which is critical, since estate taxes are likely to rise significantly in the future.

Warren, Bill, and You

Can you afford to contribute now, not just when you die? The traditional amount of contributions, particularly in religious giving, has been 10 percent of income. That's a great standard, but some people may not be able to do that right out of the gate. Maybe 3 percent or 5 percent is a level you can work with at present. Perhaps the most important thing is that you are developing a regular habit of giving.

Not everyone can, or wants to, give away all of their money before they die. Two exceptions are Warren Buffett and Bill Gates, who should be greatly commended for their generosity. The rest of us can look for a number that is specific to us. Instead of Buffett's or Gates's $30 billion, it may be $300,000, $30,000, or a larger or smaller figure. But if you want to leave a legacy, look for creative ways to give now. However, for many people, leaving a legacy through insurance remains the most feasible option.

Donor-Advised Funds

One of the great developments for charitable giving in the past few decades is the donor-advised fund. Fidelity runs one, as do Schwab and several other major institutions. Many communities have their own community-run donor-advised funds housed at a local bank or foundation.

A donor-advised fund allows you to place all the money you plan to use as charitable contributions into one place. Suppose you placed $1,000 into that fund. If the local heart association asked for a donation, you could simply contact the donor-advised fund and have it write the check and send it for you. The fund employees handle all the paperwork, verifying that the recipient is a tax-deductible 501(c)(3) charity and is current on its filings. (You might also use an Internet search engine to research the charity and see if any articles surface that give you pause.) You pay the donor-advised fund 0.6 percent a year for the privilege of holding your money and then disbursing it at your instruction.[9]

Besides the great administrative value, a donor-advised fund has other advantages. If you've regularly set aside $100 each month into this account, when a charity solicits you for a donation—say, before the winter holidays—you can instruct the fund to donate $100 without worrying about that month's bills and whether you have enough for holiday gifts or other related costs. You've already set the money aside.

Donor-advised funds allow you to give anonymously, if you wish. And remaining funds in the account can even be invested to make more money until the time you decide to send donations to a charity. Also, the money can be counted as a tax deduction the minute you send it to the donor-advised fund. You do not have to wait until it is disbursed.

STRATEGY #8 Checklist

☑ Think about how you will spend your time during retirement. Ways to fill the day can include volunteering or, as discussed earlier in the book, sometimes a part-time job.

☑ If you plan on leaving money to your children, the purchase of a life insurance policy may be the best solution, as it is exempt from estate tax and passes directly to the beneficiaries.

☑ You can leave a legacy by donating to charities. Donor-advised funds are an easy way to establish a charitable account with the ability to donate to multiple charities.

Conclusion

FEAR AND PRESUMPTION ARE NOT YOUR FRIENDS

Millions of Americans are approaching retirement and are unprepared for the transition. The exact number of those people at risk is a gigantic 50 million, according to a special report published in the *Journal of Financial Planning* by a director of the National Endowment for Financial Education.[1] Of these 50 million, 70 percent live paycheck to paycheck. Because of the overwhelming portion of America now so unprepared for retirement, this scenario "poses a serious risk to the nation's economic and social well-being."[2]

This crisis is further exacerbated by another megatrend: the generation that will follow these unprepared Baby Boomers now approaching retirement is smaller in size and will therefore be unable to pick up the economic slack. This problem was brought to light largely by the work of Peter F. Drucker, world-renowned author and management consultant to global corporations. In *Management Challenges for the 21st Century*, Drucker asserts that the most important trend of the future is the collapsing birthrate in the developed world. "There is no precedent for it in all of history," he writes.

For 200 years, social scientists assumed a steadily growing population with each generation, says Drucker. But this is no longer the case. The entire developed world has a birthrate below the necessary 2.1 percent to sustain itself. Countries such as Italy are at a horrifying 0.8 percent. The United States is also below replacement level but has maintained its population so far through immigration. "Above all," says Drucker, "there is no precedent for a population structure in which old people past any traditional retirement age outnumber young people as they already do in parts of Europe and as they will do in all developed countries well before the middle of the 21st century."[3]

Among other adjustments, Drucker concludes that the retirement age will have to change to 79, "the age that, in terms of both life and health expectancies, corresponds to age 65 in 1936, when the United States, the last Western country to do so, adopted a national retirement plan (Social Security)." Any future business strategy must begin with this demographic megatrend of a collapsing birthrate. "Of all developments, it is the most spectacular, the most unexpected, and one that has no precedent whatever," he repeats.

"The birthrate collapse has tremendous political and social implications that we cannot even guess at today," Drucker concludes.[4]

PRESUME NO LONGER

If you are reading this book, you are likely one of those members of the baby boom generation. There is a high-percentage chance you are at risk regarding your retirement. If so, your goal of retirement is likely being hampered by one of the two enemies named in the Introduction: *fear* and *presumption*.

People's presumption works against them when, though they are aware of the current economic, financial, and social issues facing them, they still conclude (erroneously) that they are out of harm's way and that further retirement preparation is unnecessary, or they believe they simply cannot overcome the issues, so they give up. Since you have read up to this chapter, you now know that retirement is nothing to take for granted. Several trends now make retiring much more difficult:

◆ People save almost nothing apart from pension plans.
◆ 401(k) accounts are performing below expectations because of the human factor.
◆ Stocks and bonds are more volatile.
◆ Health care costs are increasing significantly.
◆ Life expectancy is steadily increasing.
◆ Home equity is no longer a major asset.
◆ Social Security has been modified for increased taxes and premiums as well as a later payday.

If you were under the spell of presumption before reading this book, you should now be in a position to reject such thoughts and focus on the basics. Start by finding a solid financial professional, preferably one who owes you a fiduciary standard, and develop a detailed financial plan.

DON'T BE PARALYZED BY YOUR MISCONCEPTIONS

The misconceptions covered throughout this book are easy to dissect and overcome if you pay attention to the facts and don't let fear rule your financial future. Remember the following points, implement the strategies, and start making concrete steps toward your personal and financial goals for retirement:

◆ **You are not already prepared to retire.** Half of Americans are at risk to retire unsuccessfully. Of these Americans, 28 percent believe they are in good shape to retire and are wrong. With the decline of the traditional pension plan, individuals must be more proactive in their retirement-planning process. Individual retirement accounts (IRAs), 401(k) plans, and other defined-contribution plans have become the main retirement vehicles. Social Security is meant to act as a supplement to a retiree's existing retirement funds. Annuities and long-term care insurance should be reviewed with your financial adviser. The onus is on you to start planning for your retirement.

STRATEGY: Overcome the misconceptions and chart your course.

◆ **Social Security is not on the brink of collapse.** Social Security is a debt promised to retirees by the U.S. government. That IOU will be paid as surely as Treasury bill IOUs will be paid to investors, and the IOU called a dollar bill will be legal tender in the future. Not only will Social Security checks be honored, they are and will be indexed to inflation, ensuring their purchasing power. Every serious investor should develop a comprehensive financial plan that includes Social Security as part of its future assets.

STRATEGY: Develop an overall financial plan of which Social Security is only one part.

◆ **The Fed does not skim 5 percent from the currency.** Whatever interest the Fed earns from the money it buys and sells for the U.S. Treasury is used to pay for its services to the government. The surplus left over—usually around 95 percent of the money collected—is returned to the Treasury each year. Deflation kills the economy. Therefore, a moderate inflation of 1 to 2 percent per year seems to be the agreed-upon goal for modern America, and you need to choose investments that will account for that inflation.

STRATEGY: Identify the inflation-adjusted amount you need at retirement.

◆ **Avoiding Wall Street is not a smart strategy.** While the financial institutions collectively known as "Wall Street" bring hard-hitting and complicated activity to the market-place, the trading in this world that leads to rising values in securities (profits) is a phenomenon you need to interact with in order to grow your own investment portfolio. But don't expect to negotiate this abyss by yourself. Retain a licensed financial professional who is required by law to look out for your personal financial interests above his or her own.

STRATEGY: Retain a licensed financial professional who deals with Wall Street.

◆ **Government bailouts were not targeted for the insiders.** Certainly, several of the key players in the bailouts of critical financial institutions can be traced to the institutions them-selves, such as Goldman Sachs. But the evidence shows that drastic measures were required for a drastic crisis. The bail-outs kept all of us from experiencing a far worse catastrophe.

STRATEGY: Maintain your own personal bailout fund.

◆ **Leverage is debt—and is almost always a bad idea.** Debt is extremely tempting for every American, as well as for corpo-rations, municipalities, and the federal government. While there are instances where debt is tolerable, most uses of debt, especially credit cards, can be ruinous to your retirement plan.

STRATEGY: Rather than accruing debt, accumulate savings.

◆ **Health and long-term care will not be available and free for all.** The health care system, including insurance, will require significantly higher patient contributions and/or higher fed-eral and states taxes in the future as costs rise. What's more, you and your spouse are likely to live at least 10 years longer than your grandparents.

STRATEGY: Utilize annuities and other strategies to account for longevity and health care.

◆ **There is more to the American dream than simply kicking back and never working again.** Becoming independently wealthy is the goal, but does it mean your productive life is over? We are all designed to make a difference in this life, and that calling should continue, even when an employer no longer demands your services.

   STRATEGY: Plan your legacy through children and charity.

CLOSING ACTION ITEMS

Examine the following checklist of action items discussed in this book. Are you on track for a better financial future?

☐ Retain a financial professional charged with putting your interest ahead of his or her own.

☐ Chart a comprehensive financial plan that answers the core questions regarding your goals.

☐ Determine your number—the amount of money you need to successfully retire when you stop working.

☐ Avoid any debt obligations longer than seven years, including your mortgage.

☐ Develop an emergency fund consisting of six months of your current income in liquid assets.

☐ Prepare for living a long life by utilizing annuities such as longevity insurance and long-term care insurance.

☐ Look beyond yourself to your children and to charity in order to find true fulfillment.

If you checked all seven, you are well on your way to rejecting the misconceptions and following the eight strategies. You are now doing your part to make reality, truth, and financial success a part of your future.

Notes

PREFACE

1. Jeré Longman, "World Cup Draw Incites Conspiracy Theorists," *New York Times*, Dec. 4, 2009.
2. Ibid.
3. Ronald Tillery, "Past Results Make It Seem like NBA Lottery Is Rigged," *Commercial Appeal*, May 18, 2009, http://www.commercialappeal .com/news/2009/may/18/nba-draft-lotterytuesday-night-conspiracies/ ?partner=RSS.
4. Steve Czaban, "Is It a Reach to Say the Ewing Lottery Was Fixed?" Comment 2, May 21, 2008, *OnMilwaukee.com*, http://onmilwaukee.com/ sports/articles/czabe052108.html.
5. "Was the Lottery Rigged?" True Hoop, *ESPN.com*, June 4, 2007, http://espn .go.com/blog/truehoop/post/_/id/3471/was-the-lottery-rigged.
6. Tillery, "Past Results."
7. Simon Kuper, "Azzurri's Quest Consoles Nation Rocked by Scandals," *Financial Times*, July 7, 2006, http://www.ft.com/cms/s/2/6129251e-0de3 -11db-a385-0000779e2340.html.
8. Eric Pfanner, "Once Mystery, Swiss Soccer Loss Starts to Add Up," *New York Times*, Nov. 23, 2009, http://www.nytimes.com/2009/11/24/sports/ soccer/24iht-fitt://www.nytimes.com/2009/11/.
9. "Tim Donaghy," *Wikipedia*, http://en.wikipedia.org/wiki/Tim _Donaghy#Allegations_against_the_NBA.

INTRODUCTION

1. Alicia H. Munnell, Anthony Webb, and Francesca Golub-Sass, "The National Retirement Risk Index: After the Crash," Brief no. 9-22 (Boston: Center for Retirement Research at Boston College, Oct. 2009). The

Center for Retirement Research is headquartered at Boston College and publishes the National Retirement Risk Index (NRRI) to measure the share of American households who are at risk of being unable to maintain their pre-retirement standard of living in retirement. The NRRI is derived from the Federal Reserve's Survey of Consumer Finances (SCF), a survey taken every three years to collect detailed information from representative U.S. households. Based on the most recent SCF in 2007, the NRRI calculated that 44 percent of households were at risk. However, since those figures are from before the 2008 financial meltdown, they represent "a world that no longer exists," so the Center for Retirement Research conducted significant interviews to calculate what the SCF figures would likely be for 2009. From those calculations, the center determined a new at-risk figure of 51 percent.

2. Federal Reserve Bank of St. Louis Economic Research, "Personal Saving Rate (PSAVERT)," Jan. 31, 2011, http://research.stlouisfed.org/fred2/series/PSAVERT.

3. Alicia H. Munnell, Francesca Golub-Sass, Mauricio Soto, and Anthony Webb, "Do Households Have a Good Sense of Their Retirement Preparedness?" Brief no. 8-11 (Boston: Center for Retirement Research at Boston College, Aug. 2008). The number is 28 percent and includes health care expenses in retirement.

4. Ibid. See table 6, p. 5.

STRATEGY #1

1. Susan Pulliam and Scott Thurm, "What Goes Up: For Some Executives, the Internet Dream Has a Deep Downside—an Unhappy Upper Echelon of Ex-Centimillionaires Sees Stakes Plunge 90%," *Wall Street Journal*, Oct. 20, 2000, pp. A1, A6.

2. Ibid., pp. A1, A6.

3. Alicia H. Munnell and Annika Sundén, "401(k) Plans Are Still Coming Up Short," Brief no. 43 (Boston: Center for Retirement Research at Boston College, Mar. 2006), p. 1.

4. Alicia H. Munnell and Laura Quinby, "Pension Coverage and Retirement Security," Brief no. 9-26 (Boston: Center for Retirement Research at Boston College, Dec. 2009), p. 4.

5. Ibid., p. 2.

6. Ibid., p. 3; see n. 9.

7. Munnell and Sundén, "401(k) Plans," p. 5.

8. Ibid.

9. U.S. Department of Labor, Bureau of Labor Statistics (2008), cited in Munnell and Quinby, "Pension Coverage," p. 1.

10. Munnell and Quinby, "Pension Coverage," p. 4.

11. Brent A. Neiser, "Averting At-Risk Middle America's Retirement Crisis," *Journal of Financial Planning* 22, no. 7 (July 2009): 56–57.

12. Alicia H. Munnell, Francesca Golub-Sass, and Anthony Webb, "What Moves the National Retirement Risk Index? A Look Back and an Update," Brief no. 7-1 (Boston: Center for Retirement Research at Boston College, Jan. 2007), p. 5; Glenn Ruffenach, "Have You Learned Your Lessons?" *Wall Street Journal*, Nov. 14, 2009; Munnell and Sundén, "401(k) Plans," p. 2.

13. Felicitie C. Bell and Michael L. Miller, "Life Tables for the United States Social Security Area, 1900–2100," Actuarial Study no. 120, *Actuarial Publications: Actuarial Notes and Studies* (Aug. 2005), http://www.social security.gov/OACT/NOTES/as120/LifeTables_Tbl_10.html, retrieved Feb. 17, 2011.

14. Alicia H. Munnell, "Population Aging: It's Not Just the Baby Boom," Brief no. 16 (Boston: Center for Retirement Research at Boston College, Apr. 2004), pp. 5–7.

15. Munnell, Golub-Sass, and Webb, "The National Retirement Risk Index," pp. 1, 5–7; Ruffenach, "Have You Learned Your Lessons?"

16. Alicia H. Munnell, Mauricio Soto, Anthony Webb, Francesca Golub-Sass, and Dan Muldoon, "Health Care Costs Drive Up the National Retirement Risk Index," Brief no. 8-3 (Boston: Center for Retirement Research at Boston College, Feb. 2008), p. 4.

17. Centers for Medicare and Medicaid Services, *Annual Report of the Boards of Trustees of the Federal Hospital Insurance and Federal Supplementary Medical Insurance Trust Funds* (Washington, DC: U.S. Department of Health and Human Services, 2007), as cited in Munnell et al., "Health Care Costs," pp. 2–3.

18. Munnell et al., "Health Care Costs," p. 5.

19. Ruffenach, "Have You Learned Your Lessons?"

20. Munnell, Golub-Sass, and Webb, "The National Retirement Risk Index," p. 5.

21. Munnell and Sundén, "401(k) Plans," p. 4; Ruffenach, "Have You Learned Your Lessons?"

22. Olivia S. Mitchell et al., *The Inattentive Participant: Portfolio Trading Behavior in 401(k) Plans* (Ann Arbor, MI: Michigan Retirement Research Center, University of Michigan, June 2006), p. 3, as cited in Ruffenach, "Have You Learned Your Lessons?"

23. Neiser, "Averting At-Risk Middle America's Retirement Crisis," p. 57; Ruffenach, "Have You Learned Your Lessons?"

STRATEGY #2

1. U.S. Department of the Treasury, "History of the U.S. Tax System," fact sheet, http://www.ustreas.gov/education/fact-sheets/taxes/ustax.shtml; see also "Payroll Tax," *Wikipedia*, http://en.wikipedia.org/wiki/Payroll _tax#Social_security_and_Medicare_taxes.

2. Ravi Batra, *Greenspan's Fraud* (New York: Palgrave Macmillan, 2005), p. 15.

3. 1983 Greenspan Commission on Social Security Reform, "Appendix C of the 1983 Greenspan Commission on Social Security Reform," ch. 2 (Social Security Administration, Social Security History), http://www.ssa.gov/ history/reports/gspan5.html, retrieved Mar. 17, 2006.

4. Webb, Roy H. "The Stealth Budget: Unfunded Liabilities of the Federal Government," *Economic Review* (Federal Reserve Bank of Richmond) 77, no. 2 (May/June 1991).

5. Allen W. Smith, *The Looting of Social Security* (New York: Carroll & Graf, 2003), p. 19.

6. Batra, *Greenspan's Fraud*, pp. 30–31.

7. John Attarian, "The Immorality of Social Security," *The Freeman*, Jan. 1995; Associated Press, "Social Security Expects No COLAs for 2 Years," *The Washington Post*, Aug. 24, 2009; Social Security Administration, "1990 Annual Report of the Board of Trustees of the Federal Old-Age and Survivors Insurance and Disability Insurance Trust Funds: Summary," p. 8, available at Social Security Online, http://www .ssa.gov/history/reports/trust/trustreports.html#summaries; Social Security and Medicare Boards of Trustees, "A Summary of the 2009 Annual Reports," Social Security Online: Status of the Social Security and Medicare Programs, http://www.ssa.gov/OACT/TRSUM/index .html.

8. Allan Sloan, "Next in Line for a Bailout: Social Security," *Fortune*, Feb. 2, 2010, as cited in David Nicklaus, "Social Security Moves from Surplus to Deficit This Year," *St. Louis Post-Dispatch*, Feb. 4, 2010.

9. A. Haeworth Robertson, *Social Security: What Every Taxpayer Should Know* (Washington, DC: Retirement Policy Institute, 1993).

10. Jim Cramer on "Mad Money," CNBC, Dec. 17, 2008, quoted in Jeff Poor, "Cramer: Social Security a Bigger Ponzi Scheme than Madoff's," *Business & Media Institute*, Dec. 18, 2008.

11. Tom Gorman, *The Complete Idiot's Guide to Economics* (Indianapolis, IN: Alpha, 2003).

12. Clark Burdick and Lynn Fisher, "Social Security Cost-of-Living Adjustments and the Consumer Price Index," *Social Security Bulletin* 67, no. 3 (2007), http://www.ssa.gov/policy/docs/ssb/v67n3/v67n3p73.html.

13. Sloan, "Next in Line for a Bailout."

14. Congressional Budget Office, "The Cyclically Adjusted and Standardized Budget Measures," table 1, p. 3 (The Congress of the United States, April 2008). Retrieved from http://www.cbo.gov/ftpdocs/90xx/doc9074/04-18-StandBudget.pdf.

15. Johanna Gray and Virginia P. Reno, "Social Security Finances: Findings of the 2007 Trustees Report," *Social Security Brief*, no. 24 (National Academy of Social Insurance, Apr. 2007), http://www.nasi.org/research/2007/social-security-finances-findings-2007-trustees-report.

16. "2010 United States Federal Budget," *Wikipedia*, http://en.wikipedia.org/wiki/2010_United_States_federal_budget#Deficit.

17. Dennis Cauchon, "Leap in U.S. Debt Hits Taxpayers with 12% More Red Ink," *USA Today*, updated May 29, 2009, http://www.usatoday.com/news/washington/2009-05-28-debt_N.htm.

18. Barbara A. Butrica, Howard M. Iams, and Karen E. Smith, "The Changing Impact of Social Security on Retirement Income in the United States," *Social Security Bulletin* 65, no. 3, table 3, 2003–2004. The actual percentage ranges from 28 to 34 percent, depending upon age.

19. Tiffany Bass Bukow, "The Importance of Financial Planning: National Financial Planning," *Bizzy Women*, June 29, 2009, http://bizzywomen.com/2009/the-importance-of-financial-planning-national-financial-planning; Shashank Nakate, "Importance of Financial Planning," *Buzzle.com*, http://www. buzzle.com/articles/importance-of-financial-planning.html.

20. For a longer list of pertinent questions related to a comprehensive financial plan, see Financial Freedom, LLC, "Why It's Critical to Have a 'Financial Roadmap,'" http://www.finfree.com/FFcompfinplan.html.

21. "Information About Your Statement," Social Security Online, http://www.socialsecurity.gov/mystatement/.

22. David A. Weaver, "The Economic Well-Being of Social Security Beneficiaries, with an Emphasis on Divorced Beneficiaries," *Social Security Bulletin* 60, no. 4 (1997); "Elizabeth Taylor," *Wikipedia*, http://en.wikipedia.org/wiki/Elizabeth_Taylor#Marriages.

STRATEGY #3

1. Lawrence H. Officer and Samuel H. Williamson, "Purchasing Power of Money in the United States from 1774 to 2009," *MeasuringWorth*, 2010, http://www.measuringworth.com/ppowerus. According to *MeasuringWorth*, $1 in 1913 had the purchasing power of $22.35 in 2009.

2. Patrick J. Buchanan, "Saving Professor Bernanke," *Human Events*, Jan. 26, 2010.

3. Aaron Russo, transcript of video interview, *Our World in Balance*, http://ourworldinbalance.blogspot.com/2006/07/story-of-aaron-russo.html. Video can be viewed at Google Videos, http://video.google.com/videoplay?docid=-3254488777215293198#.

4. Ron Paul, "The Time Has Come: Let's End the Fed," transcript of address to Congress, Feb. 25, 2008, *RonPaul.com*, http://www.ronpaul.com/2009-02-26/the-time-has-come-lets-end-the-fed.

5. Dennis Cauchon, "Leap in U.S. Debt Hits Taxpayers with 12% More Red Ink," *USA Today*, updated May 29, 2009, http://www.usatoday.com/news/washington/2009-05-28-debt_N.htm.

6. Jeanne Sahadi, "$4.8 Trillion: Interest on U.S. Debt," *CNN Money*, Dec. 20, 2009, http://money.cnn.com/2009/11/19/news/economy/debt_interest/index.htm?cnn. Interest will be equal to a third of expected tax revenues by 2015.

7. "Benjamin Franklin," *Wikiquote*, http://en.wikiquote.org/wiki/Benjamin_Franklin. This alleged quote by Franklin, along with the two following, are prevalent misquotes. See Strategy section following this misconception for the actual Franklin quote that was misinterpreted.

8. "Thomas Jefferson," *Wikiquote*, http://en.wikiquote.org/wiki/Thomas_Jefferson.

9. "Alexander Hamilton," *American Experience*, PBS, http://www.pbs.org/wgbh/amex/hamilton/peopleevents/e_bank.html.

10. This theory is widely espoused on the Internet. For one example, see "The 'U.S.' Bank," *Reformation Online*, http://www.reformation.org/usbank.html.

11. "Money," *Awaken to the Truth*, http://www.awakentothetruth.com/money.html.

12. Martin Van Buren, *The Autobiography of Martin Van Buren*, vol. 2 of *Annual Report of the American Historical Association for the Year 1918*, ed. John Clement Fitzpatrick (Washington, DC: U.S. Government Printing Office, 1920), chap. 43, p. 625.

13. Minutes of the Philadelphia committee of citizens sent to meet with President Jackson, Feb. 1834, cited in Stan V. Henkels, *Andrew Jackson and the Bank of the United States: An Interesting Bit of History Concerning "Old Hickory"* (privately printed, 1928).

14. Mike Hewitt, "America's Forgotten War Against the Central Banks," *Market Oracle*, Oct. 21, 2007, http://www.marketoracle.co.uk/Article2522.html.

15. Liberty-Tree.ca, "Quote from Abraham Lincoln," Famous Quotations/Quotes, http://quotes.liberty-tree.ca/quote/abraham_lincoln_quote_b712.

16. G. Edward Griffin, *The Creature from Jekyll Island: A Second Look at the Federal Reserve* (Westlake Village, CA: American Media, 1994), p. 357.

17. Aaron Russo, Video Interview with Conscious Media Network. Aaron Russo on America: From Freedom to Fascism. April 1, 2006. Retrieved from http://www.youtube.com/watch?v=G_S48fWd69w.

18. "Audit the Federal Reserve," RonPaul.com (fan site), 2009–2010, http://www.ronpaul.com/congress/legislation/111th-congress-200910/audit-the-federal-reserve-hr-1207.

19. Matt Taibbi, "The Big Takeover" *Rolling Stone*, Apr. 2, 2009.

20. Ibid.

21. "H.R. 1207: Federal Reserve Transparency Act of 2009," *GovTrack.us*, http://www.govtrack.us/congress/bill.xpd?bill=h111-1207.

22. Jeanne Cummings, "Bailout Payout Tops $8 Trillion," *Politico*, Dec. 16, 2008. http://www.politico.com/news/stories/1208/16620.html.

23. Ron Paul, *End the Fed* (New York: Grand Central Publishing, 2009), p. 174.

24. Ibid., p. 141.

25. "Woodrow Wilson Quotes: Excerpt from 1912 Campaign Speech," Woodrow Wilson Presidential Library and Museum, http://www.woodrowwilson.org/learn_sub/learn_sub_show.htm?doc_id=472697.

26. "Executive Order 11110," *Wikipedia*, http://en.wikipedia.org/wiki/Executive_Order_11110.

27. "Benjamin Franklin," *Wikiquote*.

28. G. Thomas Woodward, *Money and the Federal Reserve System: Myth and Reality*, CRS Report for Congress, no. 96-672 E (Washington, DC: Congressional Research Service, Library of Congress, July 31, 1996), pp. 14–15, available at http://upload.wikipedia.org/wikipedia/commons/6/6a/CRS_FRBSF_Myth_Reality.PDF; Edward Flaherty, "Debunking the Federal Reserve Conspiracy Theories (and Other Financial Myths)," updated Sept. 5, 2000, available at http://famguardian.org/Subjects/MoneyBanking/FederalReserve/FRconspire/FRconspire.htm.

29. "Federal Reserve System," *Wikipedia*, http://en.wikipedia.org/wiki/Federal_Reserve_System.

30. "Money," *Wikiquote*, http://en.wikiquote.org/wiki/Money.

31. Woodrow Wilson Presidential Library, "Woodrow Wilson Quotes."

32. Linda Lowell, "Viewpoint: You'd Think the Fed Was the Bastille," *HousingWire*, Sept. 24, 2009, http://www.housingwire.com/2009/09/24/you%E2%80%99d-think-the-fed-was-the-bastille.

33. Ron Paul, "Fed Up," *Forbes*, May 15, 2009, http://www.forbes.com/2009/05/15/audit-the-fed-opinions-contributors-ron-paul.html.

34. Lee Eisenberg, *The Number* (New York: Free Press, 2006).

35. Alicia H. Munnell, Francesca Golub-Sass, and Anthony Webb, "What Moves the National Retirement Risk Index? A Look Back and an Update," Brief no. 7-1 (Boston: Center for Retirement Research at Boston College, Jan. 2007), p. 7.

36. Alicia H. Munnell, Anthony Webb, and Francesca Golub-Sass, "The National Retirement Risk Index: After the Crash," Brief no. 9-22 (Boston: Center for Retirement Research at Boston College, Oct. 2009).

37. Tom Lauricella, "Retiring? Pay Off Your Mortgage," *Wall Street Journal*, Aug. 18, 2009, http://finance.yahoo.com/focus-retirement/article/107534/retiring-pay-off-your-mortgage.html?mod=fidelity-readytoretire.

38. Munnell, Golub-Sass, and Webb, "The National Retirement Risk Index," p. 5; Glenn Ruffenach, "Have You Learned Your Lessons?" *Wall Street Journal*, Nov. 14, 2009.

STRATEGY #4

1. Leah Nathans Spiro, "Goldman Sachs: How Public Is This IPO?" *BusinessWeek Online*, May 17, 1999, http://www.businessweek.com/1999/99_20/b3629102.htm. For an explanation of an initial public offering (IPO) and a list of all IPOs of the past few years, along with their underwriters, see "Initial Public Offering (IPO)," *Wikinvest*, http://www.wikinvest.com/wiki/Initial_Public_Offering_(IPO).

2. "A Historical View of Culture Change at Goldman Sachs," *GoldmanSachs666.com*, Feb. 23, 2010, http://www.goldmansachs666.com/2010/02/historical-view-of-culture-change-at.html.

3. Matt Taibbi, "The Great American Bubble Machine," *Rolling Stone*, July 9–23, 2009.

4. Ibid. This article by Matt Taibbi—widely read, popular, and controversial—is used extensively in the Misconception section of the chapter.

5. David Usborne, "Goldman Sachs Cited in Wall Street IPO Scandal," *The Independent*, May 14, 2002, http://www.independent.co.uk/news/business/news/goldman-sachs-cited-in-wall-street-ipo-scandal-651111.html. One of the first articles on Goldman Sachs and laddering.

6. David Glovin, "Banks to Settle Internet IPO Suit for $586 Million," *Bloomberg.com*, http://www.bloomberg.com/apps/news?pid=news archive&sid=awfbdX.RY6gM.

7. Patrick McGeehan, "Panel's Report Offers Details on 'Spinning' of New Stocks," *New York Times*, Oct. 3, 2002, http://www.nytimes.com/2002/10/03/ business/panel-s-report-offers-details-on-spinning-of-new-stocks.html. This is an interesting and brief article on the panel's report, including Meg Whitman and "spinning."

8. Stephen Labaton, "Wall Street Settlement: The Overview; 10 Wall Street Firms Reach Settlement in Analyst Inquiry," *New York Times*, Apr. 29, 2003, http://www.nytimes.com/2003/04/29/business/wall-street-settlement-over-view-10-wall-st-firms-reach-settlement-analyst.html.

This article breaks down the entire settlement (for all 10 firms involved) this way: $375.5 million in restitution, $487.5 million in penalties, $432.5 million to pay for independent research, and $80 million for investor education.

9. "Dot-com Bubble," *Wikipedia*, http://en.wikipedia.org/wiki/Dot -com_bubble.

10. David Rynecki, "Goldman Sachs Withdraws Public Offering," *USA Today*, September 29, 1998, p. 1B. This announcement mentions Jon Corzine's and Henry Paulson's roles as co-CEOs of the company in the wake of this IPO withdrawal.

11. "ABC News" explained CDOs as follows: "In one group of mortgages— say 1,000 homes—40 or so might not be paying on time. But the profits you make off the other 960 mortgages will offset any losses you suffer from those 40 bad loans." Scott Mayerowitz, "ECON 101: Credit Crunch for Dummies," *ABC News*, Mar. 20, 2008, http://abcnews.go.com/Busi ness/Economy/story?id=4482623&page=2. See also "Collateralized Debt Obligation (CDO)," *Wikinvest*, http://www.wikinvest.com/wiki/ Collateralized_debt_obligation_(CDO).

12. Brooksley Born, interviewed on "The Warning," *Frontline*, PBS, October 20, 2009, http://www.pbs.org/wgbh/pages/frontline/warning/ interviews/born.html.

13. Taibbi, "The Great American Bubble Machine."

14. F. William Engdahl, "Perhaps 60% of Today's Oil Price Is Pure Speculation," *Global Research* (Centre for Research on Globalization), May 2, 2008, http://www.globalresearch.ca/index.php?context=va&aid=8878.

15. Taibbi, "The Great American Bubble Machine."

16. James R. White et al., *Tax Administration: Comparison of the Reported Tax Liabilities of Foreign- and U.S.-Controlled Corporations, 1998–2005*, GAO-08-957 (Washington, DC: U.S. Government Accountability Office, July 24, 2008), http://www.gao.gov/new.items/d08957.pdf.

17. "The History of the Stock Market," http://www.hermes-press.com/ wshist1.htm.

18. Federal Deposit Insurance Corporation, "Insured or Not Insured? A Guide to What Is and Is Not Protected by FDIC Insurance," Deposit Insurance, http://fdic.gov/consumers/consumer/information/fdiciorn .html; see also first paragraph of "Federal Deposit Insurance Corporation," *Wikipedia*, http://en.wikipedia.org/wiki/Federal_Deposit _Insurance_Corporation.

19. Donna Smith, "Study Shows Most Corporations Pay No U.S. Income Taxes," Reuters, Aug. 12, 2008, http://www.reuters.com/article/idUSN 1249465 620080812.

20. Ibid.

21. Schwab, "New Schwab Data Indicates Use of Advice and Professionally-Managed Portfolios Results in Higher Rate of Return for 401(k) Participants," press release, Nov. 28, 2007.

22. DALBAR, Inc., *Quantitative Analysis of Investor Behavior, 2009*, DALBAR, Inc., p. 4.

23. Brent A. Neiser, "Averting At-Risk Middle America's Retirement Crisis," *Journal of Financial Planning* 22, no. 7 (July 2009): 56–57.

24. Glenn Ruffenach, "Have You Learned Your Lessons?" *Wall Street Journal*, Nov. 14, 2009.

25. Sarah Holden and Jack VanDerhei, "401(k) Plan Asset Allocation Account Balances, and Loan Activity in 2004," Issue Brief 272 (Washington, DC: Employee Benefit Research Institute, 2005), cited in Alicia H. Munnell and Annika Sundén, "401(k) Plans Are Still Coming Up Short," Brief no. 43 (Boston: Center for Retirement Research at Boston College, Mar. 2006), p. 4.

26. Munnell and Sundén, "401(k) Plans," p. 4.

27. Ruffenach, "Have You Learned Your Lessons?"

28. Liz Pulliam Weston, "Can You Trust Your Financial Advisor?" *MSN Money*, undated, http://articles.moneycentral.msn.com/Retirement andWills/CreateaPlan/CanYouTrustYourFinancialAdviser.aspx.

29. David Serchuk, "Suitability: Where Brokers Fail," *Forbes*, June 24, 2009.

30. Weston, "Can You Trust Your Financial Advisor?"

STRATEGY #5

1. For a good definition and overview of the CDS, see "Credit Default Swap (CDS)," *Wikinvest*, http://www.wikinvest.com/wiki/Credit_Default _Swap_(CDS).

2. Andy Serwer, "No. 22 Henry Paulson, Goldman Sachs," *Fortune*, Aug. 11, 2003, http://money.cnn.com/magazines/fortune/fortune_archive/2003/ 08/11/346841/index.htm (article on Hank Paulson's tenure as CEO of Goldman Sachs); "Henry Paulson," *Wikipedia*, http://en.wikipedia.org/ wiki/Henry_Paulson#Goldman_Sachs.

3. Gerald Seib, "In Crisis, Opportunity for Obama," *Wall Street Journal*, Nov. 21, 2008, p. A2, available at http://online.wsj.com/article/SB122 721278056345271.html.

4. Greg Kaufmann, "Friedmanism at the Fed," *The Nation*, Feb. 25, 2010, http://www.thenation.com/doc/20100315/kaufmann.

5. Michael Daly, "Pin AIG Woes on Brooklyn Boy: Joseph Cassano Walked Away with $315 Million While Company Staggered," *New York Daily News*, March 17, 2009, http://www.nydailynews.com/money/2009/03/17/2009-03 -17_pin_aig_woes_on_brooklyn_boy_joseph_cass-1.html.

6. Anna Schecter, Brian Ross, and Justin Rood, "The Executive Who Brought Down AIG," *ABC News Online*, Mar. 30, 2009, http://abcnews.go.com/Blotter/story?id=7210007&page=1.

7. Matt Taibbi, "The Big Takeover" *Rolling Stone*, Apr. 2, 2009.

8. Ibid.

9. Center for Responsive Politics, "Top Contributors to Barack Obama," *OpenSecrets.org*, http://www.opensecrets.org/pres08/contrib.php?cycle=2008&cid=n00009638.

10. Taibbi, "The Big Takeover."

11. Federal Trade Commission, "Before You File for Personal Bankruptcy: Information About Credit Counseling and Debtor Education," Facts for Consumers, Nov. 2006, http://www.ftc.gov/bcp/edu/pubs/consumer/credit/cre41.shtm.

12. "Bankruptcy Pros and Cons," *ConsumerAffairs.com*, http://www.consumeraffairs.com/finance/bankruptcy_02.html.

13. Federal Trade Commission, "Before You File for Personal Bankruptcy: Information About Credit Counseling and Debtor Education," Facts for Consumers, Nov. 2006, http://www.ftc.gov/bcp/edu/pubs/consumer/credit/cre41.shtm.

14. "Bank Run," *TheFreeDictionary*, http://financial-dictionary.thefreedictionary.com/run+on+the+bank.

15. "Fractional-Reserve Banking," *Wikipedia*, http://en.wikipedia.org/wiki/Fractional-reserve_banking.

16. Eric Dinallo, "What I Learned at the AIG Meltdown," *Wall Street Journal*, Feb. 2, 2010.

17. Ibid.

18. Gary Thayer, *The Week* (Wells Fargo Advisors), Dec. 21. 2009, http://www.jgpgroup.wfadv.com/files/8087/theweek%2012.21.2009.pdf.

19. Scott Lanman, "Friedman Quits Fed on Concern over Goldman Sachs Ties," *Bloomberg.com*, May 8, 2009, http://www.bloomberg.com/apps/news?pid=20601110&sid=a68WNA7cKzu8.

20. Ibid.

21. Catherine Arnst, "Study Links Medical Costs and Personal Bankruptcy," *Bloomberg Businessweek*, June 4, 2009, http://www.businessweek.com/print/bwdaily/dnflash/content/jun2009/db2009064_666715.

STRATEGY #6

1. "How to Get Rich with Credit Card Debt," *Money Matador*, July 2, 2006, http://www.moneymatador.com/2006/07/02/how-to-get-rich-with-credit-card-debt.

2. CarletonSheets.com, "Real Profit$ in Real Estate," http://www.carleton sheets.com/online-real-estate-program.

3. Peter S. Goodman, "This Is the Sound of a Bubble Bursting," *New York Times*, Dec. 23, 2007, http://www.nytimes.com/2007/12/23/business/23 house.html?pagewanted=4&%23&_r=1.

4. Adam Milton, "Leverage Is Good, and More Leverage Is Very Good," *About.com*, http://daytrading.about.com/od/daytradingbasics/qt/ Leverage.htm.

5. Kerry A. Dolan, "Inside a Billionaire's Real Estate Troubles," *Forbes*, May 29, 2008, http://www.forbes.com/2008/05/29/blixseth-yellow stone-housing-forbeslife-cx_kd_0529realestate.html; Amy Wallace, "Checkmate at the Yellowstone Club," *New York Times*, June 13, 2009, http://www.nytimes.com/2009/06/14/business/14yellow.html?_r =1&ref=business.

6. Cited in Andrew Beattie, "Should You Pay in Cash?" *Investopedia*, undated, http://www.investopedia.com/articles/pf/08/pay-in-cash.asp ?viewed=1.

7. Wallace, "Checkmate at the Yellowstone Club."

8. Goodman, "This Is the Sound of a Bubble Bursting."

9. All Burkett quotes are from Larry Burkett, *Debt-Free Living: How to Get Out of Debt (and Stay Out)* (Chicago: Moody Press, 1989).

10. U.S. Census Bureau, "Housing: Financial Characteristics," Sept. 17, 2004, *American FactFinder*, http://factfinder.census.gov/jsp/saff/SAFF Info.jsp?_pageId=tp14_housing_financial.

11. "Mortgage Loan," *Wikipedia*, http://en.wikipedia.org/wiki/Mort gage_loan.

12. "What Is the Average Length of a Mortgage?" *Answers.com*, http://wiki .answers.com/Q/What_is_the_average_length_of_a_mortgage.

13. Richard K. Green and Susan M. Wachter, "The American Mortgage in Historical and International Context," *Journal of Economic Perspectives* 19, no. 4 (Fall 2005): 93–114.

14. Ibid.

15. Liz Pulliam Weston, "The Hidden Costs of Homeownership," *MSN Money*, undated, http://moneycentral.msn.com/content/banking/home buyingguide/p37628.asp.

16. Robert Longley, "Lifetime Earnings Soar with Education," *About.com*, Feb. 13, 2010, http://usgovinfo.about.com/od/moneymatters/a/edand earnings.htm.

17. Carol Hymowitz, "Any College Will Do," *Barron's*, Sept. 18, 2006.

18. "U.S. Code, Title 11, Chapter 5, Subchapter II, § 523, Exceptions to Discharge," Legal Information Institute, Cornell University Law School, http://www.law.cornell.edu/uscode/11/523.html.

19. "Cost per Semester for Attending Harvard University?" *Answers.com*, http://wiki.answers.com/Q/Cost_per_semester_for_attending _Harvard_University.

20. Joshua Kennon, "Warren Buffett Biography: The Story of Berkshire Hathaway's Billionaire Chairman," *About.com: Investing for Beginners*, http://beginnersinvest.about.com/cs/warrenbuffett/a/aawarrenbio.htm.

21. University of Nebraska–Lincoln, "Student Accounts: 2009–10 Academic Year Tuition Rates and Explanation of Fees," http://stuaccts.unl .edu/tuition-fee/tandfa0910.shtml.

22. "Credit Slips: A Discussion on Credit and Bankruptcy," *CreditSlips.org*, Feb. 12, 2008 (thread's original post).

23. David Henry, "The Time Bomb in Corporate Debt," *Business Week*, July 15, 2009.

24. U.S. Department of the Treasury, Bureau of the Public Debt, "The Debt to the Penny and Who Holds It," TreasuryDirect.gov, http://www.treasury direct.gov/NP/BPDLogin?application=np.

25. Defeat the Debt, "Understanding the Danger, Recognizing the Danger," http://defeatthedebt.com/understanding-the-danger/recog nizing-the-danger/.

26. David Walker, interview on "Ten Trillion and Counting," *Frontline*, PBS, posted Mar. 24, 2009, http://www.pbs.org/wgbh/pages/frontline/ten trillion/interviews/walker.html.

27. Ibid.

28. Paul O'Neill, interview on "Ten Trillion and Counting," *Frontline*, PBS, posted Mar. 24, 2009, http://www.pbs.org/wgbh/pages/frontline/ten trillion/interviews/oneill.html.

29. North Texas Tollway Authority, "About Our Roadways: The Dallas North Tollway (DNT)," http://www.ntta.org/AboutUs/Roadways/Road ways.htm.

30. Employee Benefit Research Institute, *EBRI Databook on Employee Benefits*, chap. 4, updated Apr. 2010, http://www.ebri.org/pdf/pub lications/books/databook/DB.Chapter%2004.pdf.

31. Alicia H. Munnell and Annika Sundén, "401(k) Plans Are Still Coming Up Short," Brief no. 43 (Boston: Center for Retirement Research at Boston College, Mar. 2006), p. 5; Alicia H. Munnell and Laura Quinby, "Pension Coverage and Retirement Security," Brief no. 9-26 (Boston: Center for Retirement Research at Boston College, Dec. 2009), pp. 1, 5.

32. Munnell and Quinby, "Pension Coverage," p. 4; Munnell and Sundén, "401(k) Plans," p. 2.

33. Ibid.

34. Laura Lallos, "YourEncore Keeps Retirees in the Game," *Business Week*, Apr. 15, 2010.

STRATEGY #7

1. Associated Press, "Obama to Sign Health Bill, Take It on the Road," MSNBC.com, Mar. 23, 2010, http://www.msnbc.msn.com/id/35982527/ ns/politics-health_care_reform/.
2. David Morales, "Health Reform: A Success Story—More Massachusetts Residents Have Health Insurance," *Commonwealth Conversations: Public Health*, Dec. 14, 2010, http://publichealth.blog.state.ma.us/2010/12/ health-reform-a-success-story-more-massachusetts-residents-have -health-insurance-.html.
3. David Leonhardt, "Health Cuts with Little Effect on Care," *New York Times*, Dec. 29, 2009, http://www.nytimes.com/2009/12/30/business/ economy/30leonhardt.html?_r=3&ref=global.
4. Arnold Relman, review of *Tracking Medicine: A Researcher's Quest to Understand Health Care*, by John E. Wennberg, *New York Review of Books*, Sept. 30, 2010, http://www.nybooks.com/articles/archives/2010/sep/30/ health-care-disquieting-truth/?page=1#fn5-200982500.
5. Shawn Tully, "Five Painful Health-Care Lessons from Massachusetts," *Fortune*, June 16, 2010, http://money.cnn.com/2010/06/15/news/economy/ massachusetts_healthcare_reform.fortune/index.htm.
6. Ibid.
7. "Section 6E. The governor shall recommend, the general court shall enact, and the governor shall approve a general appropriation bill which shall constitute a balanced budget for the commonwealth. No supplementary appropriation bill shall be approved by the governor which would cause the state budget for any fiscal year not to be balanced." 2006 Massachusetts Code, Chapter 29, Section 6E, General appropriation bill; balanced budget.
8. Robert J. Samuelson, "As Massachusetts Health 'Reform' Goes, So Could Go Obamacare," *Washington Post*, July 18, 2010, http://www.wash ingtonpost.com/wp-dyn/content/article/2010/07/18/AR2010071802733 .html.
9. Atul Gawande, "The Cost Conundrum," *New Yorker*, June 1, 2009, http:// www.newyorker.com/reporting/2009/06/01/090601fa_fact_gawande.
10. Ibid.
11. Ibid.
12. Society of Actuaries, *Key Findings and Issues; Longevity: The Underlying Driver of Retirement Risk; 2005 Risks and Process of Retirement Survey Report* (Schaumburg, IL: Society of Actuaries, July 2006), table, "U.S. Life Expectancies at Birth, Ages 65 and 85," p. 16.
13. Ibid., table, "Probability of Survival from Age 65 to 80, 90, and 100—a Technical Perspective," p. 17.
14. Ibid., p. 18.

15. Glenn Ruffenach, "Have You Learned Your Lessons?" *Wall Street Journal*, Nov. 14, 2009.
16. Ibid.

STRATEGY #8

1. "Frederick Jackson Turner: The Significance of the Frontier in American History, 1893," *Modern History Sourcebook*, http://www.fordham.edu/halsall/mod/1893turner.html; "Frederick Jackson Turner," *Wikipedia*, http://en.wikipedia.org/wiki/Frederick_Jackson_Turner; Frederick Jackson Turner, *The Frontier in American History* (New York: Holt, 1921).
2. The idea that Jefferson used "property" instead of "happiness" in an early draft of the Declaration of Independence appears to be "mythical." See discussion in "John Locke vs. Thomas Jefferson, Why Did Jefferson Omit 'Property'?" *Objectivism Online Forum*, http://forum.objectivismonline.net/index.php?s=5d3de231028b9f9e2309388c9f8c685f&showtopic=13747&st=0&p=189694&#en try189694.
3. Rush Limbaugh, "In Defense of Individualism" (transcript), *Rush Limbaugh.com*, Mar. 20, 2009, http://www.rushlimbaugh.com/home/daily/site_032009/content/01125113.guest.html.
4. Ibid.
5. Ibid.
6. Joan K. Morris, Derek G. Cook, and A. Gerald Shaper, "Loss of Employment and Mortality," *British Medical Journal* (Apr. 30, 1994).
7. Ecclesiastes 2:1-11 (NIV).
8. The author's father-in-law, a very smart guy.
9. See Fidelity Charitable Gift Fund, Internet home page, http://www.charitablegift.org.

CONCLUSION

1. Brent A. Neiser, "Averting At-Risk Middle America's Retirement Crisis," *Journal of Financial Planning* 22, no. 7 (July 2009): 56–57, statistics from p. 58.
2. Ibid., p. 57.
3. Peter F. Drucker, *Management Challenges for the 21st Century* (New York: HarperCollins, 1999), pp. 44–45.
4. Ibid., pp. 46–51.

Index